FORGOTTEN SUMMERS

Sept 7, 1995

Donald M. Kington

FORGOTTEN SUMMERS

The Story of the

Citizens' Military Training Camps

1921-1940

☆ ☆ ☆
★ ★ ★

TWO DECADES PUBLISHING

SAN FRANCISCO

Two Decades Publishing
Box 167, 3739 Balboa Street
San Francisco, California 94121

Manufactured in the United States of America

First Edition

ISBN: 0-9645789-0-5

Library of Congress catalog card number 95-061004

This history of the
Citizens' Military Training Camps
is dedicated not only to
those nearly 200 CMTC alumni
who helped make the book possible,
but to the other many thousands
who in their youth voluntarily devoted
a month of one summer—and often
more—to the challenges
and satisfactions of soldiering.

★ CONTENTS ★

Mention CMTC (Citizens' Military Training Camps) today and people are more likely to recall the CCC (Civilian Conservation Corps), a shorter lived, far better known, and entirely different program.

My military service began in 1951, 10 years after the demise of CMTC; thus, I was only vaguely aware of the existence of the program. It was in 1975 while serving at Headquarters, Second ROTC Region, Fort Knox, Kentucky, that the long-dead program took on new life for me. As I was making early preparations for the public affairs operation at the 1975 ROTC Basic Camp that summer, I received a copy of *The Mess Kit*, a yearbook from a 1925 CMTC conducted at what was then "Camp" Knox. My longtime friend, Frederick Nichols, an attorney from my home-town of Madisonville, Kentucky, had acquired the book and sent it on to me. The book contained names and hometowns of the nearly 2,500 young men who trained at Knox during a sweltering July in 1925.

The 1975 ROTC Basic Camp was to be unique. Women would attend for the first time and receive—also for the first time—to-tally integrated training. Although a year before a small number of women had attended the Advanced Camp at Fort Riley, Kansas, the training they had received was separate and modified. The Basic Camp's special status and the serendipity of discovering the existence of the camp held a half-century earlier prompted the idea of organizing a 50th year reunion of those who attended the 1925 camp.

Publicity efforts within the former Fifth U.S. Army Corps Area (Indiana, Kentucky, Ohio, and West Virginia) to locate CMTC alumni were surprisingly productive. Plans for the reunion proceeded and during the first week in July almost 50 CMTC alumni from the 1920s returned to Knox where they spent two days touring the post and observing college-age men and women train together in basic military skills.

As we prepared for the reunion, I did some casual research into the subject of CMTC and learned that no comprehensive, detailed history of the program had ever been published. I half promised myself that one day I would attempt to fill that gap by documenting CMTC's history with a book.

After retiring from active duty in 1978, the idea of attempting a CMTC history became a half-*forgotten* promise, as I became engrossed in a second career as a public relations officer for Bank of America in San Francisco. Then in 1988 a letter to the editor in *Army Magazine* written by Maj. Gen. David Gray, U.S. Army (Retired), in which he referred to his CMTC experiences, renewed my interest in the project. I wrote to the general, who quickly responded and furnished me with valuable recollections of his one year of CMTC. He also urged me to begin work on the book and not wait until I retired a second time. It was then that I began sending locator items to various military publications requesting information on CMTC and responses from its alumni.

Each of those who responded was sent a questionnaire asking for details about his CMTC experience, reactions, and reminiscences about the program. The response was gratifying. At the end of four years I had collected more than 220 names, with 185 of them returning the questionnaire or providing detailed information. Many sent CMTC documents, photos, clippings, medals, and insignia—some of it lent and much of it donated. All of this was in addition to the materials, letters, and oral comments I received from those responding to or attending the 1975 CMTC reunion at Fort Knox.

In several cases I heard from surviving relatives of former CMTC candidates. The list of those responding represented attendees of all 20 years of the program. Naturally the larger percentage of those who responded attended the last four or five years of the camps.

The returned questionnaires contained interesting, informative, and sometimes amusing information about the camps and the era in which they were held. In all they represented a priceless oral history that is woven throughout this recounting of CMTC's 20-year period. It is this oral history that, I believe, brings to life the story of the Citizens' Military Training Camps.

San Francisco   *D.M.K.*
April 1995

You see no beauty in the parched parade,
The quivering, heat-glazed highways mile on mile,
The fields where beauty holds a debt unpaid,
The gray, drab barracks in monotonous, grim file.

You take no joy when dust wraiths dimly curl
Above the winding column crawling on far hills.
You see but short beyond the present whirl
Of circumstance, your little wrongs and petty ills.

But when it all has passed and you have lost
The swinging rhythmic cadence of the marching feet,
Then you will reck as paltry small the cost,
And memory will purge the bitter from the sweet.

Prophecy, by Robert P. Warren

P*rophecy* was written in 1922 by a 17-year-old Kentuckian while attending one of the new Citizens' Military Training Camps (CMTC)—this one at Camp Knox, Kentucky, a half-day's train ride from the young man's hometown of Guthrie. It was Robert P. Warren's first year at camp and the second year for CMTC.

Later, using his full name, Robert Penn Warren, the young man became one of America's most eminent men of letters, winning three Pulitzer Prizes—one for fiction and two for poetry—as well as being named America's first official poet laureate.

CMTC would continue for another 18 years until it was dropped to make way for the nation's mobilization in the face of the threat from the Axis powers. Except for the dwindling number of veterans of the month-long voluntary summer camps, this 20-year program of military training is all but forgotten. And yet, at its height in the late 1920s, almost 40,000 young men attended some 50 Citizens' Military Training Camps located throughout the nation.

The CMTC alumni who lent their memories to this book, including Warren himself, were virtually unanimous in saying that their time at camp—whether they attended only one or all four of the years offered—had special meaning to them and later paid valuable dividends.

Thus, seventeen-year-old Warren showed amazing prescience when he wrote in the final line of his aptly titled poem: *"And memory will purge the bitter from the sweet."**

---

*The subsequent publicity for the 50th year reunion of the 1925 Camp Knox CMTC turned up a 1922 edition of the CMTC annual, *The Mess Kit*. This edition appears to have been the first yearbook published for the Knox camp. It was in this book that I discovered Robert Penn Warren's poem *Prophecy*. I contacted Mr. Warren by letter to confirm that he was indeed the Robert P. Warren who composed *Prophecy*. I soon received the following note, scrawled in vibrant red ballpoint:

March 6, 1975

Dear Colonel Kington,

Even if the poem is as awful as it is, I can't deny paternity. But I had, mercifully, forgotten all about it.

About the poem but not about the summer, which meant something to me.

As for the greetings to the reunion—by all means.

Even if I had never been the target of a shot fired in anger I do know what a Kentucky sun can do in July. So warmest regards to all, & I hope all shoulders could still bear the weight of a Springfield.

Warm regards to you too, sir.

Yours,

Robert Penn Warren

Several years later, in an interview with the *Los Angeles Times*, Mr. Warren said that *Prophecy* (written at Camp Knox when he was 17) was the first poem he had ever written.

At the time of my correspondence with Mr. Warren, James A. Grimshaw, Jr. was putting together a bibliography of Warren's works. Warren informed him of the discovery of the poem. It is the first Warren poem listed in Grimshaw's *Robert Penn Warren, A Descriptive Bibliography, 1922–79*, published by the University Press of Virginia, Charlottesville, 1981.

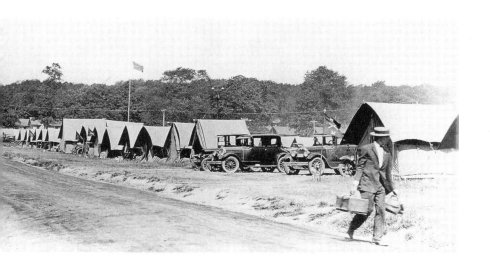

The Seed Is Planted

1 9 1 3 — 1 9 2 0

The parentage of the Citizens' Military Training Camps was never in doubt. CMTC clearly was the offspring of the War Department and the influential Military Training Camps Association—with Congress playing midwife. But the infant program wasn't quite what any of the three had envisioned during its gestation period.

The authority for conducting CMTC was the National Defense Act of 1920, signed into law by President Woodrow Wilson on June 4, 1920. Section 47 of the 1916 National Defense Act had created CMTC, along with the Reserve Officers' Training Corps (ROTC), but the war in Europe had postponed CMTC's implementation.

The actual seed for establishing a training program for young civilians, however, was planted in the summer of 1913 when the Army conducted two experimental camps for college men. General Leonard Wood was Chief of Staff. It was Wood's political and public-relations savvy that launched the fledgling attempt at military preparedness.[1]

The idea of summer military training for civilians wasn't new. For years the militia had conducted camps of instruction. A supplement to the 1912 War Department Annual Report had recommended summer camps in conjunction with a proposed national reserve organization.[2]

The inspiration for Wood's actions in 1913 came from a situation that is unimaginable in modern-day Army protocol.

During Cornell University's spring break Lt. Henry T. Bull, the university's professor of military science, took the train from Ithaca, New York, to Washington and quickly obtained an audience with the chief of staff.[3]

Bull had learned of the Navy's plan to offer college students a two-month summer cruise aboard battleships and thought the idea could be adapted by the Army. He proposed to Wood that qualified students be attached to Regular Army units for four or five weeks in the summer, but strictly as volunteer civilians, with no enlistment involved.

Wood liked the idea but believed special camps should be established for the training. He assigned Bull to a three-officer committee to prepare a detailed program. The other two officers were Captain Robert O. Van Horn and Captain Douglas MacArthur. More than 20 years later MacArthur would again play important roles in the Army's summer training program for young civilians.

With the backing of Lindley M. Garrison, Secretary of War in the new Wilson administration, Wood sent the following circular to the presidents of colleges and universities throughout the nation:

1. The Secretary of War has decided to hold two experimental military camps of instruction for students of educational institutions during the coming summer vacation period. Should these camps prove a success, it is intended to hold them annually, one in each of the four sections of the country.

2. The object of these camps is, primarily, to increase the present inadequate personnel of the trained military reserve of the United States by a class of men from whom, in time of national emergency, a large proportion of the commissioned officers will probably be drawn, and upon whose military judgment at such time, the lives of many other men will in a measure depend.[4]

Maj. Gen. Leonard Wood, attributed by many to have been the U.S. Army's first effective chief of staff, was the driving force behind the Plattsburg Movement in his single-minded campaign for national defense prior to World War I. (National Archives.)

Despite the short notice and limited time for preparation, two successful camps were conducted that summer—one in Gettysburg, Pennsylvania, for the Eastern sector and one for the West in Pacific Grove, California, near the Presidio of Monterey.

There were no extra appropriations for the camps, nor did Wood attempt to obtain any. In addition to transportation costs to and from camp, the training cost for each young man was $27.50: $10 for uniforms and $17.50 for food.[5]

The camps were so successful that the next year four camps were scheduled. The 1914 camps were located in Ludington,

Michigan, near the shores of Lake Michigan; Asheville, North Carolina, near the Pisgah Mountains; and Fort Ethan Allen, Vermont, on Lake Champlain. The camp in the West remained in the Monterey area.[6]

By 1915 the European continent was engulfed in war, causing the idea of military preparedness to take on a new urgency for Americans. This concern was particularly strong in New York and other urban areas of the Northeast. Influential young Eastern executives and politicians became so anxious about the issue that they, almost spontaneously, helped create what became known as the "Plattsburg Movement."

Hundreds of distinguished and not-so-distinguished public and private leaders in their thirties and forties, including the 36-year-old mayor of New York City, John Purroy Mitchel, volunteered for a summer camp at Plattsburg Barracks in upstate New York.[7] This camp was in addition to the camps for college men, which continued in 1915. The four-week training at Plattsburg was officially known as the Business Men's Camp but was branded early and irrevocably by the press as the "Tired Business Men's Camp."*

Although the camp's extensive publicity, particularly in the New York newspapers, concentrated on the lighter side, it sharpened the nation's new awareness of the preparedness movement.

One of the nation's most vocal and distinguished proponents

---

*The reader might question the spelling of "Plattsburg" since the city's official spelling is now "Platts*burgh*." From *Briefly Told*, a history of the city written in 1984 by Dr. Allan S. Everest, and furnished by the Clinton County Historical Association, Plattsburgh: "All of the early usage included the 'h' at the end—town, village and city were incorporated that way. Yet during the 19th century many people dropped the letter as a kind of abbreviation. In 1892 the Postmaster General deleted the 'h' on all of the towns in the country (U.S.) except Pittsburgh. As far as the federal government was concerned, the town's name had no 'h' until 1955 when the Postmaster General, in response to local agitation, officially designated the city as 'Plattsburgh,' which most citizens had supposed it was all along."

of military readiness took to his "bully pulpit" to express his enthusiastic support of summer military training for young men. Theodore Roosevelt said: "The military tent, where boys sleep side by side, will rank next to the public school among the great agents of democracy."[8]

The graduates of the 1915 and 1916 camps gave the spark for the formation of the Military Training Camps Association (MTCA), with the core of its membership principally alumni of Plattsburg training.[9]

The MTCA soon gained sufficient political clout to influence Congress's approval of a full appropriation for the 1917 camps. In April, however, the nation declared war against Germany, wiping out any possibility of summer camps for volunteer civilians. The MTCA quickly suggested to the Secretary of War that the proposed civilian camps be converted into officers' training camps. The association and the War Department carried on a nationwide recruiting campaign, and by August 27, 341 candidates had graduated from the first series of officers' training camps. This, wrote the Secretary of War, was a number sufficient to meet the immediate needs of the Army."[10]

The Officers' Candidate Schools ran from May 1917 through November 1918 at locations across the nation. Officer candidates, after careful screening, were given three months of intensive training. By May and June of 1918, 57,307 graduates from the first three series of schools had been commissioned and enrolled in the new National Army. At the time of the Armistice in November about 46,000 candidates were enrolled in the fourth and last series of officers' schools. Because of the need for officers of all grades, commissions were granted up to the rank of colonel in the first two series. In 1917, 297 officers' school graduates were commissioned as field grade officers, including two full colonels. The camps also provided a sizeable number of captains and first lieutenants.[11]

An officers' candidate camp for African Americans also was

opened in June 1918 at Fort Des Moines, Iowa. By October of that year the camp had commissioned 639 black officers, all in the Infantry.[12]

Marked indelibly with the sarcastic sobriquet of "90-day Wonders"—a nickname later inherited by the graduates of Officers' Candidate Schools during World War II—graduates of this quickly improvised World War I training program provided the Army with a cadre of combat leaders unsurpassed in any of the nation's previous wars.

As essential as this military-preparedness training was to the Army's success—actually its *very survival* in Europe—the concept would always have its detractors.

In *The Top Kick,* Leonard H. Nason's gritty and often darkly humorous novel set on the battlefields of France, two of the Regular Army doughboys, both of whom apparently had been cadre at Plattsburg Barracks, have the following conversation: ". . . I aim to get a commission out of this scrap and it's time I was after it."

"Well, you would 'a' got one at Plattsburg if you hadn't gone givin' your opinion on them sheep-herdin' jaspers they called reserve officers. You wouldn't expect to get a commission after tellin' a bunch o' millionaires they wouldn't make a pimple on a good soldier's nose, would yuh?"[13]

How many millionaires attended Plattsburg or were members of the MTCA is problematic and beside the point. The MTCA was an organization made up of individuals from all over the nation who were sincerely dedicated to the idea of military preparedness—some of whom were in high enough positions to influence the Army and the Congress.

Even with the considerable influence the MTCA had by 1920, it was unable to overcome the political realities brought on by the tide of isolationist and pacifist sympathies engulfing the nation two years after the "War to End All Wars." The MTCA had vigorously campaigned for a system of universal compulsory military training.[14] Although the Senate passed a bill establishing universal military training it was rejected by the House and failed to survive in conference. The compromise bill did, at least, provide for a summer training program for American youth—the volunteer, no-further-obligation Citizens' Military Training Camps.

Although CMTC wasn't precisely the program the MTCA had fought for, the association acknowledged its parental obligation. For the next 20 years the association would promote, protect, and fight for CMTC, accepting it as something of definite value, if not quite the creation of its dreams.

The Beginning

1921

Francis McCann reported to Camp Devens, Massachusetts, on August 1, 1921—the day of his 16th birthday. The young man from Chelsea, a suburb north of Boston, was one of several hundred volunteers reporting to the camp for a month of military training.[1] These young citizen soldiers were from the six New England states making up the U.S. Army First Corps Area, and became charter members of First Corps' initial Citizens' Military Training Camp.

That same day 31-year-old Thomas Ryan reported to Fort Snelling, Minnesota, on the outskirts of Minneapolis and St. Paul, to take part in the fort's CMTC debut.[2] Ryan, who came from Randolph, a village about 35 miles south of the Twin Cities, joined 598 other young men from five of the Seventh Corps Area's eight Midwestern states.

Few of those attending CMTC's first summer could have differed much more than did McCann and Ryan. McCann was among the youngest, officially, allowed to attend. He was between his sophomore and junior years at Chelsea High School, and, although there is no record of it, judging from the way he took to the training he may have been in the Junior ROTC at Chelsea High.

In several letters home to "Ma," each one signed with his family pet name, "Boyo," McCann was enthusiastic about the training and not in the least modest about his accomplishments as a cadet leader. In two letters he expressed the universal craving of students

Francis McCann, shown here in his Naval Academy midshipman's uniform, was a 16-year-old charter member of CMTC in 1921—its first year. He graduated from the Academy at Annapolis in 1927. (Photo courtesy of his son, John C. McCann.)

and soldiers—food packages from home. "Did you receive any letter requesting pie, cake, candy, etc.?" he queried in an early letter. Later he wrote, "I received the things from the bakery and I thank you from the bottom of my heart. Believe me, it was not money wasted."

Although war veterans, and even some active duty soldiers (allowed by the congressional act), were enrolled that year in CMTC, 31-year-old Thomas Ryan hadn't served in the Great War. It wasn't because he hadn't tried. Four younger brothers and three brothers-in-law had served, but Ryan, because he worked for the U.S. Post Office Railway Mail Service and was married with an infant son, was exempt.

But in 1921 Ryan finally had a chance to do some soldiering, at least in the summer. Ryan was fortunate to have signed up in 1921, since the following year the age range for first-year men was changed to 17 to 25 from the original 16 to 35.[3]

Despite their differences in age and mode of life, McCann and Ryan had one strong similarity other than their Irish heritage; each had an aptitude for things military. After high school, McCann entered the U.S. Naval Academy from which he graduated in 1927. He retired as a Navy captain after 30-years' duty. Ryan went on to complete the CMTC course and was commissioned a second lieutenant in the Officers' Reserve Corps. He later joined the Minnesota National Guard, was called to active duty in the national mobilization of 1941, served on active duty until 1946, and in 1950 retired from the U.S. Army Reserve with the rank of major.

The legislation that gave McCann and Ryan the opportunity to soldier during that summer of 1921 was a single, albeit long, paragraph of the 1920 amendment to the 1916 act. Section 47d, titled, "Training Camps," authorized the Secretary of War, in broad terms, "to maintain, upon military reservations or elsewhere, schools or camps" for military instruction. One of the few specific details in the section authorized round-trip travel allowances of five cents a mile and, in a later amendment, a subsistence allowance of one cent a mile when transportation was furnished "in kind," i.e. when a train or bus ticket was issued by the Army.[4]

The final sentence of Section 47d put the General Staff to work determining what CMTC was to be and how it would work: "The Secretary of War is authorized further to prescribe the courses of theoretical and practical instruction to be pursued by persons attending the camps authorized by this section; to fix the periods during which such camps shall be maintained; to prescribe rules and regulations for the government thereof; and to employ thereat officers, warrant officers, and enlisted men of the Regular Army in such numbers and upon such duties as he may designate."[5]

Early the next year the Army published Special Regulations No. 44b, dated February 23, 1921, establishing details on the conduct of the camps. The camps would be of 30 days, or one month, duration. The dates for camps scheduled for the nine U.S. Army corps areas would be set by each corps commander, generally beginning in July or August. Attendance was voluntary and "without cost" to those attending, which, of course, meant there was

Thomas Ryan was a 31-year-old CMTC candidate at Fort Snelling, Minnesota, in 1921. He earned a commission in the Organized Reserve Corps by completing the three years that were required at the time. (Photo courtesy of his son, Col. William A. Ryan.)

no pay other than reimbursement for transportation. The candidates would be housed, fed, and supplied with uniforms and necessary equipment just as any Regular Army recruit.[6]

Initially, the complete CMTC course was designed to be of three summers' duration, with the first year designated as "Red," the second "White," and the third "Blue." Successful completion of the Blue course would put a young man on the way to becoming a second lieutenant in the Officers' Reserve Corps. For 1921 the training would be limited, officially at least, to the Red course comprised of infantry drill, rifle marksmanship, guard duty, camping and marching, care of equipment, personal hygiene, military courtesy, athletic contests, and military ceremonies. In actual practice at many of the camps, military veterans and youths with some type of ROTC or other military training were treated as second- or third-year men.

The Annual Report of the Adjutant General for fiscal year 1921, ended June 30, provided, in future tense, some details of the camps' conduct: "Instruction is to be provided by selected Regular Army officers. Medical officers, chaplains, and hostesses will be in attendance. No educational qualifications are required, except that the applicant's intelligence must be such as will permit him to understand and obey commands. The candidate must be of good moral character." The report went on in some detail as to physical standards and examinations.[7]

By the early spring of 1921 the general public was becoming aware of the new summer camp plan. In a headline reading "PICK WAR TRAINING CAMPS, Nine Corps Areas Expect to Instruct 9,800 Citizens in Summer" the New York Times reported a War Department announcement saying each corps area was to train approximately 1,200 men.[8] "Of the three grades of camps, 'red,' 'white' and 'blue,' the first, it was said, will be emphasized because it should appeal particularly to men between the ages of 16 and 19 and demonstrate to parents the 'physical, moral and mental development that results from military training.'" The story went on to list 16 camps that were under consideration as sites for the summer training.

On the West Coast at the Ninth Corps Area's Presidio of San Francisco and Camp Lewis, Washington, the earliest Citizens' Military Training Camps to begin that first year were into their final week, having started on July 6.[9] During the first week of training at the Presidio little if any note was taken by San Francisco's newspapers of the inauguration of the nation's first Citizens' Military Training Camp. The Sunday, July 10, *Examiner,* however, in a brief story on the inside pages, reported that attendance at the Presidio camp had been raised to 712, with an extra 113 volunteers "summoned by wire and expected to be on hand on Monday." In the same issue, but given a more prominent position and more column inches, was a profile on Maj. Gen. William M. Wright, the newly arrived commander of the Ninth Corps Area. The story also mentioned—without comment on the unusual military nepotism involved—the general's aide-de-camp, Lt. William M. Wright, Jr.[10]

Brief as it was, the *Examiner*'s CMTC story did provide a few more details: "The lads at camp have had an exciting non-military time [during] the first three days of camp seeking 'pie stretchers,' chasing 'cake levelers' and looking for the 'key to the parade ground.'. . . From now on, however, fun will be minimized and the regular training increased."

The Saturday before the West Coast camps began, newspapers across the country reported Jack Dempsey's knocking out George Carpentier of France in the fourth round of their Friday, July 1, fight at Boyle's Thirty Acres. It was the first major prizefight broadcast over that still-infant phenomenon, radio. Considering the limited number of broadcast stations and home receivers, it is unlikely the listening audience numbered anywhere near the crowd at the fight, which provided boxing's first million-dollar gate.

Just as did hundreds of newspapers across the country, the Sunday *Examiner's* "funny-papers" featured the battles of Maggie and Jiggs in the comic strip, *Bringing up Father; Snuffy Smith's* forerunner, *Take Barney Google F'instance*; and the comics' early career woman, *Tillie the Toiler.*

With the passage of Prohibition in 1920, the United States had been "dry" for a year and a new illicit industry, bootlegging, was coming into its own.

Americans were packing movie houses to see Rudolph Valentino in *The Sheik* and Mary Pickford in *Little Lord Fauntleroy.* The latest in sheet music that might be found on the parlor piano included the piano solo, "Kitten on the Keys," and hit songs, "Peggy O'Neil" and "The Sheik of Araby," which wasn't from the movie, but out of the soon-forgotten Broadway musical, *Make It Snappy.*

The day after the camps at Camp Devens and Fort Snelling began, Enrico Caruso, the world-famous tenor, died in his native Naples. "But his voice was not stilled," news stories reported at the time. Caruso had made more than 160 records for the Victor Talking Machine Company.

Even though CMTC couldn't compete with Dempsey or Caruso for the attention of the nation's press, in June newspapers ran a government press release quoting President Harding, who urged every young man to attend the new military training camps.[11]

Chances are that most of the nearly 41,000 who applied for the 12 camps had done so months before Harding's statement. And perhaps no one had told the president the Army could only accept a little more than 25 percent of those who applied.

The 11,202 men who were accepted to become CMTC "pioneers" that first summer came from all walks of life—students, farmers, clerks, the unemployed, and government workers.* There were even a number, impossible to calculate, who had served in World War I. Rear Adm. Richard ("Red") Patterson, an alumnus of the 1921 Plattsburg CMTC, said one CMTC company at Plattsburg Barracks was made up of older men, many of them veterans, including Sam Drebbin, a scout for General Pershing during the Mexican border fracas of 1916–1917.

★

As Maj. Gen. Wright assumed command of Ninth Corps Area in San Francisco another War Department assignment of more national importance and prominence was made. On July 1, 1921, General of the Armies John J. ("Black Jack") Pershing was appointed U.S. Army Chief of Staff, replacing General Peyton March. In his first two months as chief of staff, Pershing clearly demonstrated that he, and therefore the Army's General Staff, didn't look on CMTC as a stepchild. In August he visited 7 of the 12 camp sites. Back in Washington he released a statement expressing his enthusiasm for the camps, and calling for attendance to be increased to 40,000 men the next year.[12]

Pershing's 1922 goal proved too ambitious, but it was more realistic than President Harding's target of a camp attendance of

---

*The 1921 CMTC Yearbook of Ft. Snelling listed all the candidates' names, as well as their hometown and occupation. In addition to students, who were in the majority, a wide variety of occupations of the day were listed.

Maj. Gen. Peyton March, Gen. Pershing's predecessor as Army Chief of Staff, probably held the distinction of being the last U.S. Army officer to wear a beard. (National Archives.)

100,000 men a year,[13] a number that was never to be realized. Ironically, had Congress and the War Department been bold enough almost 40,000 might have attended that first year. The War Department reported 40,679 applications received, with 11,202 of the applicants approved to attend, of whom 9,973 completed the course.[14]

In addition to the five camps mentioned earlier—Devens, Plattsburg, Snelling, the Presidio of San Francisco, and Lewis—Citizens' Military Training Camps in 1921 were held in these locations: Camp Meade, Maryland (Third Corps Area); Camp Jackson, South Carolina (Fourth Corps Area); Camp Knox, Kentucky (Fifth Corps Area); Camp Grant, Illinois (Sixth Corps Area); Camp Pike, Arkansas (Seventh Corps Area); and Fort Logan, Colorado, and Camp Travis, Texas (Eighth Corps Area).[15]

On his August 1921 inspection tour, Pershing visited all six camps east of the Mississippi and ventured west of the big river only the few miles it takes to reach Fort Snelling. The Fort Snelling CMTC 1921 yearbook reported on and published three photographs of the

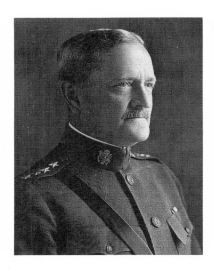

General of the Armies John J. ("Black Jack") Pershing became Chief of Staff of the U.S. Army on July 1, 1921, replacing Gen. Peyton March. (National Archives.)

battalion review held for Pershing on Wednesday, August 10. The yearbook also carried an excerpt from his address to the troops, probably remarks that changed little at all seven camps.

Assuming Candidate Thomas Ryan was close enough to the reviewing stand (public address systems were yet to come) he might have been able to hear General Black Jack say: "I hope all of you young men can return at the end of this camp and tell your fathers and mothers that you had a clean good time, that all of you, you and your mates, lived clean and moral lives. . . . You are getting more than a military training here. For you are getting an insight into the obligations that fall upon you as a citizen of the Republic."[16]

Growing Pains

1922

In its first year CMTC was well publicized, if the *New York Times* can be used as an accurate gauge. In July and August of 1921, 18 editions of the *Times* ran items on the camps, many of the August items covering daily activities at Plattsburg.[1] Few of the nation's newspapers could have matched the active interest that the *Times* took in CMTC. Consideration has to be given, of course, to the fact that Julius Ochs Adler, the newspaper's general manager and a nephew of publisher Adolph Ochs, was a colonel in the Organized Reserve Corps (and a general in World War II). An alumnus of the pre-World War I Plattsburg camps, he was an active member of the MTCA, civilian aide to the Secretary of War for New York State in the 1930s, and commanded CMTC battalions at Plattsburg and Camp Dix, New Jersey, from the mid-1920s into the 1930s.[2] For 20 years the *Times* would publicize CMTC and the MTCA to an extent that would make any public relations practitioner salivate.

A successful publicity campaign surely contributed to the more than 40,000 CMTC applications the Army received in the first year. That very success, however, led to serious recruiting problems in 1922. Only one out of four of those who applied for the 1921 camps was accepted, resulting in a high level of disappointment, even resentment, among both the rejected applicants and the civic leaders who helped with recruiting.

In 1922 Congress appropriated sufficient money for the War

Department to more than double the attendance and the number of training sites—28 camps with a total attendance of from 27,000 to 30,000. But by early June only about 17,000 applications had been received, even though recruiting efforts began a month earlier than the year before.[3]

The negative attitude encountered throughout the country perhaps was reflected in two letters received by the Second Corps recruiting officer at Governors Island, New York. One Army recruiter wrote that men who applied the year before refused to apply again. "The Chamber of Commerce, which was very active last year, refused to take any action. As soon as I mentioned Citizens' Camps to the newspapers I met a chilly atmosphere. . . . Everyone who was active last year seemed to be sore because of the method of handling the applicants."[4]

A staff member of a junior military academy, who was also a member of the Officers' Reserve Corps, wrote: "Last year I sent in the names of 18 cadets from [the writer's academy] when this camp was first advertised. Only two were chosen. If you will guarantee that the cadets who apply will be allowed to go, I will send in names, but I am unwilling to disappoint them again."[5]

At Plattsburg about 60 percent of the first-year men returned for the second-year White course, but failed to bring along the friends they had promised the year before. Evidently some feared that if they signed up a buddy, the friend might be accepted instead of them. Some, after learning of the high number turned down the year before, felt they didn't want to encourage friends to apply and then have the friends rejected.[6]

Oversubscription in 1921, apparently an intentional tactic by the Army, did have a positive side. The avalanche of applications helped convince Congress to increase appropriations so that CMTC training capacity could be almost tripled. In 1922 when a corps area's recruiting quota was met it would notify those involved in recruiting that all further applicants would be listed as alternates.[7]

Also in 1922, the CMTC program broke the bounds of the continental U.S., with a camp established in Porto Rico—the official spelling of Puerto Rico until 1932. The 28 locations selected by the War Department included what appeared to be 19 additional posts, with 3 of the 1921 posts—Jackson, Grant, and Pike—having been dropped.[8] To be precise, the new locations only numbered 18, since one on the list, Fort Scott, California, was located within the Presidio of San Francisco.

The range in age for first-year men was narrowed to ages 17 to 25 from the original 16 to 35. The age limit for the second-year White course was set at 18 to 26 years. However, no Red graduate (the first-year course) was barred on account of age.[9]

The raising of the minimum age to 17 was attributed to the War Department's being influenced by the criticism of "some of the most prominent educators and trainers of the American youth" who believed 16-year-olds shouldn't be sent to training camp with "more mature men." Prohibiting 16-year-olds from attending was another excuse given for the poor CMTC recruiting results in 1922.[10]

There is evidence, however, that Army officials often looked the other way when enforcing the age limit. At least 10 percent of those CMTC alumni who contributed their memories to this book were 16 or younger (two were only 14) when they attended their first camp.

Four years after the entry age was increased to 17 the assistant adjutant at the 1925 CMTC at Camp Knox, Kentucky, wrote:

"The age variations might also be mentioned. There were 158 boys sixteen; 977 seventeen; 624 eighteen; 342 nineteen; 187 twenty; 85 twenty-one; 40 twenty-two; 28 twenty-three; 23 twenty-four; and a few representing each other age up to thirty. . . ."[11]

In some cases the Army may have waived the age limit when the parents signed a consent form. In many cases the applicant falsified his date of birth, and the Army often didn't ask for proof of age. The late Theodore Conway, who retired as an Army four-star general, attended four years of CMTC at Camp Del Monte in Monterey, California. At his first camp in 1924 he was only 15. His father, a captain in the 30th Infantry at the Presidio of San Francisco and part of the CMTC cadre, brought young Conway with him the first two years as a "guest" candidate.

The low response to recruiting in 1922 in one way seems to have been beneficial: only a few applicants were rejected, most of whom were turned down for physical or age reasons.[12] This tended to diminish the residual bitterness that oversubscription the year before had created.

A total of about 27,000 applications had reached the Nine Corps Area headquarters by the end of June. Of that number, 22,119 men completed the 28 camps.[13] Never again in the remaining 18 years of CMTC would a paucity of applications be the cause of the program's not progressively growing. Inadequate appropriations and the Army's limited resources were the impediments that kept President Harding's goal of 100,000 participants a year from ever reaching even half that number.

The earliest camps to open in 1922 again were in the West. On Thursday, July 6, the Presidio of San Francisco welcomed the first group. The 1,000-plus candidates were slated to be trained in either Infantry, Cavalry, Field Artillery, Engineers, Signal Corps, or Air Service.[14] That same week a few hundred men reported to Fort Scott, the "post-within-a-post" at the Presidio, where a Coast Artillery branch camp was set up.

The *New York Times* again took up its unofficial role as a major publicity medium for CMTC.[15] The newspaper reported the Plattsburg camp "swamped" with candidates. Plattsburg, perennially the most popular location with Second Corps CMTC applicants, hadn't suffered from the tough recruiting year.

With Camp Dix, New Jersey, beginning its first CMTC, the *Times* looked closer to home and gave the bulk of its coverage to the training at Dix. A dispatch from Camp Dix reported: "Five hundred young Americans from New York, New Jersey, and Delaware got away for a fine start in opening today the civilian military training camp [*sic*] of the Second Corps area. The student soldiers at Camp Dix are to specialize in cavalry and engineering branches."[16]

Three days later the *Times'* correspondent reported on Saturday's review: "With briar scratches, stiffened muscles and blistered feet from their work of campaigning over the Camp Dix terrain, students from CMTC marched in their first review today on the historic parade grounds where hundreds of thousands drilled for the World War."[17] The editors even gave space to a special 1,200-word feature on the Camp Dix CMTC written by a member of the cadre, lst Lt. Herbert B. Mayer.[18] And on August 22, the *Times* reported that CMTC troops from Camp Meade, Maryland, were reviewed by President Harding and staff. There the President repeated his call for 100,000 to be trained each year.[19]

Dr. F. B. McNutt, who attended the 1922 Camp Meade training, recalled the event: "All or a portion of the CMTC contingent performed in a review near Washington Monument" for President Harding, Secretary of War John Weeks, and General Pershing. McNutt said that a squad member standing next to him was addressed by Pershing, apparently as the general inspected the line.

Any doubts about how much interest the government had in its new military training program should have faded when the nation's Commander in Chief and War Department leaders gave this sort of attention to CMTC.

The Camp Knox 1922 CMTC yearbook, *The Mess Kit,* provides a feel and flavor of what more than 20,000 young Americans experienced that summer. The book is replete with contributions from both candidates and the camp's staff members. "The Making of a CMTC Soldier" by Cadet Lt. Henry H. Gibson from Making,

Kentucky, began: "From Kentucky, Ohio, Indiana and West Virginia, we came. Some of us desirous of renewing camp life of World War days; others anxious to play the army game for a month and get an idea of what the boys of 1918 went through, and at the same time prepare ourselves for future national emergencies."[20]

In "History of Second Squadron Air Service," Cadet Cpl. Edward T. Lyons from Indianapolis, Indiana, documented the significant presence of veterans attending CMTC: "From the Blues, Earl V. Kennedy [Lakewood, Ohio], who spent two years in France as gunnery sergeant with the 5th Marines, was chosen Cadet Captain. Moreover at the end of the month he was recommended as the Blue having the best record as a soldier. . . . Henry J. Pate [Shirley, Indiana], who saw service in France with the 24th Engineers was appointed commander of the second platoon. The command of the third platoon was given to Orval R. Rose [Dayton, Ohio] who was in the Air Service for two years, during which time he was stationed at the Speedway Field, Indianapolis . . . [First sergeant] went to Clifford D. Johnson [Youngstown, Ohio], who is another war veteran. Johnson was a radio instructor in the Air Service and later was an Air Service radio sergeant attached to the 59th Field Artillery and served in France with the 30th Division."[21]

Lyons' article also recounted a serious mishap. Pvt. Joseph Donisi from Macksburg, Ohio, lost his right hand from handling a "one-pounder" dud the last week of camp. Donisi, "when visited by Captains Jones, Gruber, and Wendel the next day, was cheerful and planning his future."

On the last Monday of the month's training, members of Troop A of the Cavalry course participated in a special military ceremony. In an item headlined "Wedding Bells" *The Mess Kit* reported: "Simplicity marked the wedding of Lt. Stanley E. Hathaway [he was a reserve second lieutenant from Covington, Indiana] to Miss Claire Clark, August 28, 1922. The entire Troop A were present at the ceremonies of the groom and his bride.

Present Arms was maintained while the newlyweds walked out of the 'little church around the corner' and into the waiting car."[22]

Social events, both on and off post, were always an important part of virtually every CMTC throughout the years. Laura Kelley, one of the camp's service club hostesses, wrote an article describing some of the activities provided the candidates: "The first social affair was given Saturday evening, August 5. . . . This was a dance at the Ha-wa-in Gardens, the city's [Louisville] largest and most attractive public dance hall. . . . The trip to the city and return was made by special train. The next weekend event, the following Saturday, was a boat ride and dance with Louisville girls as guests. The excursion steamer 'America' with its roomy decks and ample accommodations for a large dancing crowd, was chartered. . . . Nearly a thousand men took part in this outing. The boat stopped 12 miles up the Ohio river at Fern Grove, a beautiful spot on the Indiana side. Mess, previously prepared in the camp kitchens, was served by the hostesses and their aides, picnic fashion. The return home proved equally enjoyable, the dancing floor of the boat still crowded when the boat docked at midnight at Louisville. A special train was waiting to bring the men back to Camp Knox. Another dance was given Saturday night, August 19, at the Ha-wa-in Gardens, admirably adapted for a private military dance. . . . With plenty of partners, who were Louisville's prettiest society buds, good music and an attractive hall, the affair proved so successful that many requests were made for a repetition."[23]

The high energy and vigorous spirit of the 1922 CMTC at Camp Knox weren't limited to that year or to Camp Knox. These qualities would be well sustained throughout CMTC's 20 years of existence.

★ 4 ★

Getting Down to Business

1 9 2 1 – 1 9 4 0

It wasn't just the social occasions and the recreation that gave CMTC its special qualities. There was, of course, the training. The Army meant for that to be presented in the most effective, stimulating, and palatable way possible. The objectives of the Red Course—the first year of training at that time—as set forth by the War Department were:

> To bring together young men of all types, both native and foreign born; to develop closer national and social unity; to teach the privileges, duties, and responsibilities of American citizenship; to stimulate the interest of the youth of this country in the importance of military training, as a benefit to the individual taking such training and as an asset vital in the problem of national defense.
>
> To show the public by actual example that camp instruction of the kind contemplated will be to the liking of their sons; will develop them physically, mentally, and morally; will teach Americanism in its true sense, thus stimulating patriotism and self-discipline, resulting in greater national strength, both civil and military.
>
> To qualify young men for service in the reserves.[1]

First-year men were to receive five hours a day of military instruction, "exclusive of the time devoted to ceremonies and to physical training." Corps commanders were authorized to prescribe a maximum of one additional hour instruction in range practice. White and Blue candidates received a maximum of six hours of military instruction, with a minimum of one hour each day provided as a study period.[2]

In 1922 training was offered in nine Army branches of service—at least on paper. These were Infantry, Cavalry, Field Artillery, Coast Artillery, Corps of Engineers, Signal Corps, Air Service, Medical Department, and Motor Transportation Corps. War Department plans called for 12 of the 28 scheduled camps to offer as many as four branches. Eight of those camps were to offer Air Service.[3] Although shortages of planes and pilots at some of the camps would put a crimp in Air Service training, it is certain that Camp Lewis, Washington, had at least four DeHaviland airplanes, since the *San Francisco Call & Post* reported the planes departing the Presidio's Crissy Field on their way to participate in CMTC at Lewis.[4]

At Camp Knox about 500 candidates were assigned to three Air Service squadrons, the majority of them being first-year men. This is puzzling because, according to regulations, Red candidates were to be trained only in basic military skills and it appears that only a few candidates in any of the three courses managed to receive even a familiarization flight. Cadet Cpl. Edward Lyons of Indianapolis wrote: "[One day] the Whites and Blues were supposed to have a conference followed by aerial flights and recreation. We had the conference all right but for the most of us the flights and recreation failed to materialize. However, a few Reds and still fewer Whites and Blues—about twenty altogether—were fortunate enough to be taken up before the flights were discontinued."[5]

Equally puzzling is the Coast Artillery unit established at Camp Knox, since the nearest "shoreline" was the banks of the Ohio River 20 miles to the north. Although regulations specified that all instruction was to be practical, it is obvious that the training in Air Service and Coast Artillery at Camp Knox was mostly lecture. This may have been one of the reasons why the wide variety of branches offered at individual camps later was reduced.

Training in the Army changed little between the world wars. Austere government appropriations, the nation's pacifistic mood, and a degree of lethargy within the U.S. military establishment had all but halted the development of new weapons and modernized training doctrine. Herman ("Pat") Herst, who attended Vancouver Barracks, Washington, from 1927 through 1930, recalled traveling by truck 200 miles to Camp Lewis to practice trench warfare. The Springfield 1903, bolt action, .30-cal rifle, the French-made 75-mm howitzer, and the old "squads right and squads left" drill remained standard with the Army throughout the 1920s and for most of the 1930s.

With that in mind, the following five chapters, which describe CMTC training and administration, are mostly from the alumni's own recollections, and don't necessarily follow any chronological order.

Left, Right, Left

The transition from civilian to soldier—from mufti to military garb—invariably involves being formed in some sort of group and moved in unison, if only in a straggling "column of ducks." Thus, the first semblance of training for any military recruit is a form of close-order drill, albeit crude. From the Army's foundation in the 1770s until the late 1930s its method of dismounted movement was squad drill. Frank Kreger, who in 1934 attended Fort Thomas, Kentucky, described the old drill this way: "Squads were squads of eight men. Squad leader (corporal), six privates, and one PFC who was the second in command of the squad. The squads were not in a front line rank as today, but faced four men to front with the other four behind. In moving out, the command was: 'Squads right, March.' The squad moved out as a turn to the right. In marching we were then in a column of squads. At the time you stepped out to swing to the right, you brought your rifle up to port, then to right shoulder. First step, port arms—second step, to right shoulder. The left hand was still on the rifle. I believe it was just touching the bolt. The next step the left hand was 'smartly' swung back to left side. Boy oh boy. It is much easier today going to right shoulder arms, then marching out."

A candidate at Camp Knox in 1922 wrote this description of the first day of drill: "Fall in! Here we were in two ranks, talls with shorts, fats with leans. 'Talls on the right and carry on.' So here we were arranged according to height. Count off, one, two, three, four—front and rear rank. Squads, sections, platoons, and finally the company was formed. Cadets and non-coms were assigned to their respective places. All set. Forward march. We naturally felt very intact and at the very zenith of our military power."[1]

The candidates' aptitude for marching wasn't universal, of course. John Moale remembered that squad drill was more complicated and took longer to learn than the later, simplified drill. He said that at the Presidio of San Francisco in 1937 and the Presidio of Monterey the next year "awkward squads" were formed for the slow learners.

According to Robert Sumner, most of the candidates caught on fast: "The first two or three days were close-order drill intensive. On the evening of the third day the battalion marched by companies in line to the main post for retreat parade. Usually several companies of the 7th Infantry [Regiment, a part of the Third Infantry Division] were lining up on the field as we arrived and took our position to their left in company fronts facing the regimental commander and his staff.

"The regimental band played all the troops onto the field. The regimental adjutant took the report, gave us parade rest, announced the officer of the day, called us to attention, ordered officers, noncommissioned officers (mostly CMTC trainees), and guidons 'center' and off they went to salute the colonel with a great deal of panache. They marched well, all accompanied by the regimental marching song 'Rangers Together' (a piece of music from the movie musical *Rio Rita*). After the leaders were back in place, the colonel whose voice could be heard *clearly* the length of the parade ground, put us through the manual of arms. To the Color was sounded, the anthem played, and the retreat gun (called sunset gun by the 7th) fired, which made all of the first-year men jump. It was a World War I French 75-mm blank and we could hear the brass casing clank when the breech was opened."

Military subjects were in the morning, with the afternoon devoted exclusively to sports for the first-year men, with some leadership or tactics classes for the advanced candidates. At the close of the day at most camps on most weekdays, it was back into field uniform and fall out for a retreat ceremony. Memories of this event remained strong with many of the former candidates. "There was a very large parade ground at Plattsburg [1937], and we had daily parades with the incomparable 26th Infantry band [First Infantry Division, Plattsburg, 1931]. We were formed up into three battalions of four rifle companies each and fairly well covered the parade ground," remembered Chester Carpenter.

With the exception of camps in the north, such as Plattsburg, or camps on the West Coast, the summer weather was invariably hot, and, unless there was a late afternoon thunderstorm, the afternoon sun scorched. These conditions often brought on something every soldier fears—passing out while standing in formation. Since it happens even to veteran soldiers, CMTC candidates were especially vulnerable.

Paul Keough recalled retreat parades at Fort Devens: "Retreat parade at Devens [1939, 1940] was always in very, very hot weather and on some days prolonged for one reason or another. The ambulance was parked to the rear of the formations. If anybody passed out from the heat, nobody else moved. Stand fast at attention or parade rest. The fallen body would be picked up by the ambulance corpsmen. We developed a pride in being able to take it—in not giving up. You can do it even if you are miserably uncomfortable. I understand that in today's philosophy, this is considered archaic, stupid, brutal, and unhealthy. I think the advantages of our old system outweigh the possible health problems."

A candidate fainting during a review at Fort Des Moines, Iowa, in 1939 provided Bruce Romick a strange sight: "As I stood at attention one afternoon I turned my eyes right to be able to see the smoke come from the cannon when it was fired. Just as the

A photo taken at Camp Knox in 1925 provides an example of how quickly CMTC candidates took to dismounted drill. The entire CMTC group of more than 2,000 was formed on the parade ground on July 4, three days after their arrival, to take an oath of allegiance to the United States of America and hear an address on the stars and stripes by the camp commander. (Photo from the 1925 Camp Knox CMTC yearbook, The Mess Kit.*)*

cannon fired, one of the trainees in the next troop fainted, falling stiffly forward as if he'd been shot. The timing was amusing to see."

Donald Armstrong remembered a strange but amusing occurrence during a review at Plattsburg Barracks in the early 1920s: "A review was staged for some visiting dignitary, I've forgotten who it was, and all went well as A Company swung past the reviewing stand. I was in the front rank and was amazed as I did 'eyes right' to see a lad further down the line produce a camera and shoot the reviewing party. For all his faults, he was skillful enough to hang on to both the camera and his rifle."

Edward Randall remembered a mishap with the salute gun at Fort Brady, on Michigan's Upper Peninsula: "There was a regular private with the 2nd Infantry who we called 'Old Horse Jaw.' He was always in the guard house. He, along with his guard, armed with a 12-gauge shotgun, was detailed to fire the salute cannon at retreat. He didn't pull the leather plug from the 75-mm. The plug went ass over tin cup between the troops and the reviewing stand, and hit the Co. M bulletin board. He got another six months in the guard house."

After the first (Basic) year, candidates didn't just fall in and march—they also were expected to take their turn in leading the drill. For a novice at drilling troops this can be a challenging and, sometimes, embarrassing experience. "One of my most memorable experiences was piling my battery into an officer's backyard hedge during infantry drill. It was in the old days when our drill manual was the infantry drill regulations, or squads right. I was maneuvering my battery toward the open spaces of the parade grounds in order to give the command 'right by squads, squads right,' but it turned out to be in the wrong direction, resulting in a pile up of a mob in the officer's yard," Stan Milkowski recalled.

Ned Wiencke attended CMTC at Camp Leonard C. Hoskins, a tent camp just outside historic Fort Monroe, Virginia. "We had parades and other 'formal' activities on the parade ground inside the fort [1935]. We had to cross the moat by a wooden bridge and we were always ordered to break step when crossing the moat because 'the constant measured tread of troops would cause the bridge to collapse.' Lord knows we didn't want that to happen!"

Three CMTC alumni have vivid memories of the new drill manual, which was introduced in the late 1930s and fully adopted by 1940. CMTC alumnus Russell Eberhardt said he was a pioneer in the introduction of the new method. Eberhardt said that as a Red candidate in 1932 at Camp Pike, Arkansas, he "taught the new extended order drill [*sic*], which replaced squad drill." He said the new drill was used by the Army the next year with Civilian Conservation Corps (CCC) troops. "However, the Regular Army did not adopt this until about 1938–1939," Eberhardt recalled.*

---

*The new drill was outlined in a 1932 manual, "Tentative Infantry Drill Regulations 1932 (For Service Test Only)." The simplified drill was officially adopted with the publishing of FM 22-5, July 1, 1939.

Plattsburg alumnus Howard ("Dusty") Rhodes said 1940 "was the first year the Armed Forces adopted the current drill-formations manual, so from basic trainee to regimental commander, we all learned together."

"I learned the new drill from our cadre, the 34th Infantry [at Camp Meade in 1939] and went home to introduce it to the 111th Infantry Medical Detachment of the Pennsylvania National Guard," said Joseph Brennan.

Whether candidates liked drill and reviews, or hated both, there was one parade that was universally loved—the final CMTC review. John Middlebrooks wrote: "I still remember our final retreat parade [Fort Barrancas, Florida, 1934]. The motley crew was well trained and they wanted to show it. Squads right and squads left, and right front into line never looked better."

★ 6 ★

On the Range

The second week [Camp Knox, 1921] they took us out to Muldraugh [Range] for firing. There was a reserve major in charge of the range. Big heavy-set fellow named Blades, with a great big deep voice. There had been a lot of debate among us about the kick of the Springfield. Everybody was wondering what it would be like. I was on the first order on the firing line. First order firing and Blade got up on a scoring table and was telling about safety. He finally got to the place where he said 'ready on the right, ready on the left, load, aim, fire.' There wasn't a gun went off. Everybody was waiting to see what the guy next to him was going to do—whether it was going to kick him off the line. Then Blades said, 'Goddam bunch of Boy Scouts, I said FIRE, now goddammit FIRE.' Then we began to shoot up and down the line." That's the way Mark Eastin remembered the first time he fired the rifle with the legendary kick.

The reputation of the Army's basic weapon, the Springfield '03, embellished as it was by recruits' barracks bull sessions, generated a high level of anxiety for the first day of range firing. Stories of the rifle's mean kick weren't all latrine rumors, however. Here is what former professional soldier Victor Vogel said about the Springfield: "The regular army did not keep records of casualties inflicted on shooters by their own weapons, but these occurred in large numbers. Hardly a man left the firing line without a black eye, a bloody nose, a bruised cheek, a fractured jaw, or busted teeth. The Springfield packed tremendous power, propelling a bullet with a muzzle velocity of more than 2,800 feet per second, and the recoil would punish a man unmercifully. Many a recruit would close his eyes, grit his teeth, and jerk the trigger, dreading the impact that followed, suffering in silence until he got the hang of it through practice and proper sling adjustment, which took up most of the recoil. Still many an expert walked off the firing line with a sore jaw."[1]

Jack Ellwood remembered some candidates at the 1928 Vancouver Barracks camp being punished by the nonlethal end of the '03: "The firing range sticks out in my mind because the smaller members came off with black eyes and bloody noses from the old Springfields."

Perhaps William Huntley and his fellow candidates at the 1935 Fort Snelling camp received exceptional supervision during the dry-firing training, because his memory of the Springfield is different: "We were warned that the '03 Springfield had a strong kick. Some of us put a bath towel under our shirts to protect us from the strong kick of the rifle. We soon took the towel out because the kick wasn't that bad."

For some candidates the worst memory of the Springfield was their first encounter with it—when it was issued to them. "The rifles were in the original wooden cartons and completely smothered in cosmoline," said Alfred Freedman. Anyone who has had the job of cleaning off the black, sticky preservative will never forget the long hours involved."

The rifle range at Fort Screven, Georgia, was in an unusual setting that provided Fred Featherstone with an interesting diversion: "The post was also bordered on the north by the Savannah River and the rifle range was set up to fire through the targets, and the spent bullets would end up in the river. Red flags would warn boaters or fishermen that it was an off-limits area on firing days, but every day on the range we would hear the order to 'cease fire,' as an errant boater would then be out there in the line of fire."

Elmer Froewiss remembered the entertaining way he and his colleagues were transported to the Fort Dix rifle range in 1937:

Assuming that Camp Knox, Kentucky, had a designated safety officer in 1923, he could not have approved of the way this World War I–vintage truck was loaded. The truck apparently was on its way to or from the rifle range, but its hard-rubber-tired wheels obviously weren't moving, and none of the three men in the cab appeared to be driving the truck. Perhaps the scene was posed just for the photographer. (Photo from the 1923 Camp Knox yearbook, The Mess Kit.*)*

"The rifle range was some distance from our company area. To get there we rode a narrow gauge railroad [nicknamed the 'Dinky']. We sat on flat cars to which wooden benches had been secured. It was sort of like a ride in an amusement park."

Robert Sumner provided another cogent description of CMTC training: "For 10 days the battalion was at Camp Booneville, the rifle ranges of the 7th [Infantry Regiment]. This was about 40 miles from Vancouver and the trip was made in ton-and-a-half Chevrolet trucks driven by personnel from the Service Company. We usually went in two shuttles. No commercial-style buses, just the typical Army transportation of the day. Here we put into execution the long hours of 'dry firing' we had been taught by the cadre. We fired part of the table for qualification in the '03 rifle; 3 rounds for zero; 10 rounds slow fire and 10 rounds rapid fire. The initial firing was at the 200-yard line, then to the 300-yard line and the 500-yard line. So we shot up a lot of ammunition. There were 50 firing points and we fired from 0730 to 1100, marched back to the cantonment area, noon meal, back to the range and marksmanship until 1530 [*sic*].* One of the CMTC companies was detailed daily to operate the target butts."

Training in other shoulder-fired weapons was offered at some camps. Maj. Gen. David Gray received a lesson he never forgot while firing the Browning Automatic Rifle (BAR) at Camp Knox: "One of my lasting memories of CMTC was an occurrence when we were firing the BAR on the rifle range [1927]. I had been firing a Springfield Army rifle on the National Guard range at Evansville [Indiana] since I was 11 years old and considered myself a good shot even though I fired from my left shoulder, which made the bolt action awkward and time consuming. When it was my turn to fire I got into position with the BAR on my left shoulder. The two soldier-coaches told me I would have to fire from my right shoulder, but I stubbornly insisted on firing from the left. Finally the two soldiers turned to an officer who was sitting on a bench behind the lines. 'All right, let him fire from the left,' he growled. What I didn't realize was that with the Browning the spent shell cases were ejected more to the rear and to the right than with the Springfield, so when I pressed the trigger I got a shower of hot casings, most of which went down inside my open shirt collar—a very uncomfortable situation. I turned to see the officer observing with a sardonic gleam of satisfaction, and, without saying a word, I meekly switched to the right shoulder. To my surprise I was comfortable there, started firing from the right shoulder, easily qualified as an Expert Rifleman."

*The War Department adopted the 24-hour clock after the country entered World War II—specifically on July 1, 1942 (War Dept. Circular #187, June 13, 1942). By 1943 the U.S. Armed Forces also adopted the European calendar-date style.

A typical day on the range firing the '03 Springfield rifle. These CMTC candidates were at a range at Fort Benjamin Harrison, Indiana, sometime in the late 1930s. (Photo courtesy of Stanley L. Wolczyk.)

Some candidates' training programs called for qualifying with the Army's .45-cal automatic pistol. Robert Miller remembered the excellent training in pistol firing he received at the Presidio of Monterey in the late 1930s: "One of the best experiences was the way that the old 30th Infantry cadre taught us how to fire the .45-caliber pistol. Several days we had to hold our right arm outstretched with two water-filled canteens on a pistol belt over the right wrist. It made the automatic light in your hand, and for the dry firing and trigger squeezing exercises we put a dime just behind the front sight. If you did the right squeezing the dime stayed on the automatic, but if you jerked even a small bit then the dime would fall off. I learned my lesson well at CMTC and always qualified as an expert, thanks to the CMTC training."

Paul Keough's experience with the Army's often maligned, but

CMTC candidates at Fort Dix, New Jersey, in 1939 were treated to an entertaining ride as the fort's narrow-gauge "dinky" train transported them to the firing range. (Photo courtesy of Maj. Walter K. McEnaney.)

reliable, rifle was a motivating factor to switch to artillery: "Cleaning that damn rifle [Fort Devens, 1937, 1938] convinced me, and a couple of others, that the grass was greener in the Field Artillery," he said. "And Field Artillery was at Fort Ethan Allen, Vermont, [1939, 1940] which was that much farther away from Boston—a significant plus [i.e., more travel pay]. . . . The cadre was the 7th Field Artillery, which was motorized with 75-mm field guns. We wore britches with leggings, and cleaning the .45-caliber was less a problem than the Springfield '03. I think one of the things we liked, in comparison to Fort Devens, was the reduced formality. We'd strip to the waist in manhandling and cleaning the 75-mm guns. There was a greater team spirit in whatever we did. We were learning more practical things in the mechanics of artillery in comparison to the Infantry. . . . [July 1940] was one of the darkest for much of Europe. I suspect that was the reason we had no ammo for our 75-mm at the firing exercises [instead they rigged 37-mm on the barrel of the 75-mm]."

Donald Armstrong had these memories of artillery training: "I went on in '25 and '26 to do the White and Blue courses at Madison

Barracks. The Field Artillery was horse-drawn 75s [75-mm]. As the AEF [American Expeditionary Forces] had not had the use of any U.S.-made guns during World War I, the 75-mm, 155-mm howitzers, and 155-mm gun were all made in France. Most of the month was spent at Madison Barracks at Sackett's Harbor on Lake Ontario. But after a familiarization and drill on the guns, and some equitation, a march was made to Pine Camp [now Fort Drum] for range firing—a march of over 20 miles."

Unlike Camp Knox in 1922, with its "theoretical" Coast Artillery course, Army posts situated on sea coasts could offer the real thing. John Middlebrooks told a lively story about his Coast Artillery experience in 1935 at Fort Barrancas, Florida: "After Basic, candidates were trained to fire the 155-mm rifles at towed targets out in the Gulf. In order to have enough men to complete the gun crews, some first-year trainees were given a manual to study for several days and then given a test. Those with the highest grades were put on the gun crews. And at least 50 percent were first-year trainees. I was one of them. We trained hard and with great expectation for the day when we were to fire live ammo. We had been told all kinds of stories as to what to expect when the gun was fired. Also, you must know that we were wearing the old blue denim fatigues which were old and well worn. . . . Everyone did his job very well, but when the gun fired with a big noise and muzzle blast, half of the gun crew took off over the parapet and scattered like a covey of quail. It took about 10 minutes to get them assembled again. All had a tale to tell as to what happened to them. One had his fatigue top blown off, one had his pant leg torn up to his knee. Some said they were blown down, and some were scratched and bruised. We were all in trouble, but after it was over, it was real funny and provided many hours of enhanced conversation."

"Fort MacArthur was a Coast Artillery CMTC and the training involved harbor defense ordnance, such as 14-inch rifles, 12-inch mortars, and 155-mm guns," remembered Frank Gregory.

"When bore sighting the 14-inch it was the usual procedure to use the chimney on William Wrigley, Jr.'s [the chewing gum heir] mansion on Catalina Island."

A few camps offered antiaircraft artillery (AAA). Chester Carpenter trained in AAA at Fort Hancock, New Jersey: "Our training at Fort Hancock was quite realistic, and was infinitely more fun than close order drill and the other stuff we got at Plattsburg. We fired the .50-cal guns live several times, usually at hydrogen balloons. For our final test with the .50-cal, we fired at a towed sleeve. We also fired the 3-inch guns twice. . . . The AAA training was quite technical as, in those days, we had to learn how such things as a stereoscopic height-finder worked, and how to maintain, calibrate, and use one."

CMTC candidates on the beach at Monterey, California, fired machine guns toward Monterey Bay during their training at Camp Del Monte in 1925. This is a rare view of CMTC candidates wearing the World War I "tin pan" helmets. (National Archives.)

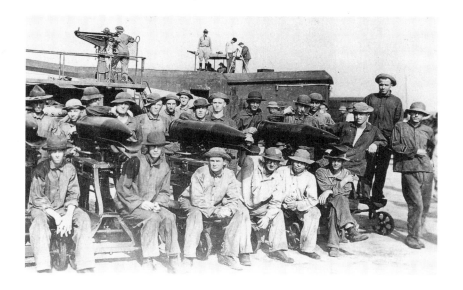

Dress was informal for CMTC candidates when training on the big guns. These lads at Fort Barrancas, Florida, in 1925, posed for the camera before target practice with 10-inch sea guns. (National Archives.)

"We fired the 3-inch AA guns dating from about 1917," said Fred Renken, who also attended Fort Hancock. "We couldn't hit a damn thing."

Several candidates who attended CMTC during its last two years, 1939 and 1940, were given a look at some of the new weapons that had finally sprung to life from the more than 20 years of moribund Army research and development. Robert Sumner recalled a demonstration in 1939 at Vancouver Barracks of the new 60-mm and 81-mm mortars, and the 37-mm anti-tank gun. "Some of us were afforded the opportunity to fire the new Garand rifle [later designated the M1] in 1940," he said. "I got to fire three rounds, rapid fire. It was a great thrill to be asked by one of the cadre to take the weapon."

Arnold Silver recalled a demonstration in 1934 at Fort Ogelthorpe, Georgia, that indicated the Army was dabbling with modernization by timing a courier on horseback against a radio message from a scout car to a point three miles away. Including the time it took for decoding the radio message, the race was a tie, Silver said.

Vivid memories such as these—all of them more than half a century old—surely indicate that the training received by these men was indeed something special.

A Touch of Tactics and
Blessed Breaks

In a four-week military training course, there isn't time to engage in elaborate war games. A few road marches and several nights of bivouac were about all the tactical training CMTC had time to schedule. Chester Carpenter remembered a field exercise, of sorts, at Plattsburg: "The third week [1937] we did what they then called 'extended order drill.' This impressed me when done on the parade field as we could deploy our platoon in a matter of seconds, so I thought we were going to be really great out there in the field. But I'll never forget my first encounter with a P-36. It swooped out from behind a mountain, dropped a big bag of colored water over the whole company, and was gone before anybody could even lift up a rifle to fire at it.

"Incidentally, the encampment under what was supposed to be battlefield conditions was amazing. We pitched pup tents according to the Infantry Drill Regulations, so many inches apart and lined up in nice straight lines; the lesson of the swooping airplane being totally ignored."

The 1925 Camp Knox CMTC yearbook carried two reports of a field exercise that may have been the one and the same. The first report: "Thursday we turned out at 3:00 A.M. with full field equipment and went to Muldraugh Range where we were the supporting battery for the Red Army. We went into action and helped the Reds secure a sweeping victory."[1]

The second report: "Then came the maneuver—a long hike,

under pack; an over-night stay in the woods; a sham battle between the Red and Blue armies; and, then the long hike back to camp. It was a new adventure for a large portion of Troop B [Cavalry] but the manner in which they conducted themselves in the sham battle is well shown in the following conversation by two infantrymen which was overheard by one of our troop.

'What did you do in the sham battle?'

'Oh, we had to stop the Cavalry.'

'Did you stop them?'

'Well, no! There was a million of them.'"[2]

In *Prophecy*, the poem that introduces this book, the imagery used by 17-year-old Robert Penn Warren perfectly portrays the drudgery and discomfort of a tactical road march. Anecdotes from two CMTC veterans also describe some of the agony involved in a long road march. "After about 24 or 25 days, much to everybody's surprise, they called for a hike," recalled Mark Eastin about his second year of CMTC at Camp Knox. "Fall out with full field equipment and armament. Rifles and all. It was the hottest damned day you can imagine. And we just kept going and kept going. Ambulances were following and every now and then someone would fall out and they'd put them in the ambulance for a while then they'd kick 'em out and put somebody else in who needed relief. And it really got to be where it was aggravating to the troops. And so the troops began to complain. 'Where we goin?' How much further is it?' We bivouacked out there somewhere in the prairie and we knew that the next day, or maybe the following day, we were going to get mustered out. So we were all dreading the march back, and the weather wasn't improving—it was bad! We weren't as fit as they must have thought we were, or as we thought we were. So they get us up early the next morning and we started this walk home, everybody dreading the hell out of it. We walked about an hour and came over a hill and there was the barracks! They'd been taking us in a circle and we didn't realize it. Boy, you talk about a bunch of guys that were happy."

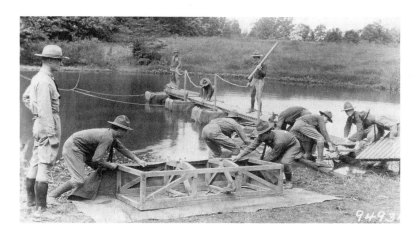

These CMTC candidates learned to build a pontoon bridge at Fort Benjamin Harrison in 1927. (National Archives.)

More than 10 years later and many hundreds of miles farther north, William Huntley and colleagues were subjected to similarly sly road-march planning by the cadre of the Fort Snelling camp: "One day they took us on a seven mile road march along the river. The road had willow underbrush along both sides. The sun was shining and the weather was sweltering. At the end of the march we bivouacked in a field. We could see our squad tents not more than a quarter of a mile from our bivouac area."

As uncomfortable as candidates were made by the blazing sun and the unaccustomed exertion, succor often came in the form of the blessed break at mid-morning. Memories of Russell Eberhardt, who attended Fort Leavenworth, Kansas, and Camp Pike, Arkansas, in the early 1930s, and Hugh Graham, an alumnus of the 1940 camp at Fort Riley, Kansas, illustrate how young, randy soldiers' minds tend to run in the same vein. "We were served milk, we called it 'titty,' and cupcakes at 10 A.M. everyday," Eberhardt said.

"I do recall after a full morning of drill or riding at 10 A.M. we had 'titty,' one-half pint of milk and a roll or donut. Sure tasted good, for growing kids," Graham remembered.

"We drilled four hours a day in the shade of the ancient oak trees, within the perimeters of the old military cemetery [Jefferson Barracks, Missouri, 1931]," said James Munday. "At our first morning break, they would serve us bottles of chocolate milk. I thought I'd died and gone to heaven!"

Norris Maxwell had an amusing memory of breaks at Fort Bliss, Texas, in the late 1930s, where the "mess sergeant brought us milk and cookies. The regulars didn't say anything, but they considered that just a bit sissy. Then one morning I happened to go around the gun shed and found our sergeants having milk and cookies out of sight. They just kind of grinned and continued eating."

Paul LaPierre and Paul Keough attended Camp Devens, Massachusetts, and Fort Ethan Allen, Vermont, a year or two apart during the late 1930s. They supplied similar accounts of refreshments from outside sources. "On the range a farmer sold us a glass of milk and a large piece of blueberry pie for 10 cents," LaPierre recalled about Fort Ethan Allen. "We passed the hat for the farmer and I was elected to give him the money. I had it in my hat and when I dumped it on the kitchen table, he passed out. We had to get him a medic to bring him out of it."

Keough, who attended Fort Ethan Allen a year after LaPierre, recalled that a number of dairy farms were located near the firing ranges: "There was a traditional standing invitation from several of the farmers' families to the CMTC city kids to drop in for fresh milk and homemade apple pie. Delicious!"

The *New York Times* reported that candidates at Camp Devens "will be milk-fed soldiers. After milk wagons had left a lot of bottles at each drill field this morning [Monday, August 4, 1924], buglers sounded an unexpected mess call and every student was required to drink a pint of fresh milk. An order from the camp commandant announced that senior officers would be required to see that each student drank a similar ration daily thereafter."[3] Could it have been that there was a strong dairy lobby around the Devens area?

James Cantwell said that at Fort Sheridan, Illinois, north of Chicago, more modern, if less wholesome, refreshments often were available in the late 1930s. He spoke of the "taste testing, when Pepsi-Cola, Cleo-Cola and other colas were furnished free for the asking. Guess they determined which was most liked by the total number of those that were asked for."

Apparently Plattsburg and Fort Hancock discontinued the humane practice of mid-morning milk breaks in the late 1930s. Chester Carpenter, who attended both camps, said: "A few years before I went to camp, it had been the policy of the Army to act as sort of boys' camp counselors and they served milk to the boys at 10 in the morning. I didn't see this, but it was so reported to us by the cadre. They, naturally, were opposed to any such mollycoddling of would-be soldiers."

★ 8 ★

The Trainers

At the core of military training is the trainer. Long after the facts of a subject have been forgotten or the acquired manual skill has gone to rust, an old soldier is apt to recall the one who taught the subject or demonstrated the skill. It seems to be the best and the worst instructors or leaders who leave an indelible imprint on the memories of those who have had military training. The CMTC alumni bear this out.

From the outset of CMTC the War Department and the civic organizations that supported the program were inclined to promote it to parents and the public as a "summer camp for boys." This theme contributed to the impression throughout CMTC's 20 years that Regular Army officers and noncommissioned officers (NCOs) were somehow transformed into avuncular Boy Scout leaders.

Although the validity of this impression remains questionable, Army directives, practices, and statements to the press gave some support to the Boy Scout camp image. The War Department's implementing directive stated: "In assigning noncommissioned officers for training and instructing candidates, care will be exercised to select only those specially fitted and qualified as to character."[1] In 1922 two San Francisco newspaper stories gave credence to the perception that CMTC youths weren't being handled the same as Regular Army recruits. A *Chronicle* story told of Lt. Col. Allen Smith, commanding officer of the camp at the

Presidio, handing out coffee and ham sandwiches to the first 400 candidates reporting.[2] From the afternoon newspaper came this story: "Jealousy has broken out in the ranks of the regular army man and all manner of politics is being worked to get assignments with the red and white army [CMTC].

"The reason for this jealousy is the unusually good 'chow' being served at the civilian camp. The regular army man does not have the quantities nor the frequency of ice cream and pie dealt to the civilian soldier and for that reason the regular army man is calling his luck all kinds of things."[3]

★

Some 60 contributors to this book—representing at least 40 camps and the two decades of the program—made specific comments about the quality of the cadre. There was consensus among them that the Regular Army NCOs were of top quality. The consensus broke down, however, when commenting on the presence or absence of a "Boy Scout atmosphere." Whether the CMTC alumni believed they were pampered or driven as hard as regular recruits, they all agreed that the leaders they encountered were competent and dedicated to giving the young Americans committed to their charge the best training possible.

A charter member of CMTC, Richard Patterson, had positive memories of the cadre he served under at Plattsburg that first year in 1921: "The captain had risen from the ranks during a 10-year career; the first lieutenant was a recent graduate of West Point and was right at home with the youthful soldiers he understood well. The top kick assigned to A Co. was a 20-year soldier—tough, demanding, understanding, and he could do anything whatsoever he ordered his trainees to try and do."

Two excerpts from a Camp Knox yearbook illustrate the affection and awe many CMTC candidates felt for their Army leaders: "Sergeant Samuel Womack—'Our Loving Sam'—Enlisted in 1899. He has been discharged eight times as a sergeant. He has been in Cuba, the Philippines and all over the U.S. . . . Has handled more rookies than any other man in the U.S.A. The First Platoon [Co. I, 10th Infantry] has a reason for calling him Loving Sam. His place in our memory will grow larger as time goes on."[4]

"When times were the blackest and we felt down and out at the mouth, as one would say, we had a good pal to cheer us up with a lot of funny jokes and entertainments. . . . Tony [Morriss, regular cadre, Co. H, 10th Infantry] couldn't be caught on any point of Army life. . . . He was the best friend that any of the fellows had in camp."[5]

More than 60 years later Maj. Gen. Gray, who in his active career observed thousands of soldiers, had this memory from his one year of CMTC at Camp Knox: "To this day I have distinct recollections of the regular soldiers of Co. K, 10th Infantry. Despite the Army, they found ways to improve the appearance of their issue uniforms. Their woolen shirts were always form fitted and in the back always had three pleats. The normally floppy campaign hat was always neatly blocked and the head strap was polished. Their breeches were washed until they acquired a soft wrinkle-proof texture and their leggings were rolled as if part of their body. . . . Some soldiers always accompanied us on practice marches and I marveled at how well they wore their field gear. Their rolls that fitted into their pack were always perfectly rolled and properly slung from their shoulders. In short, they just looked like soldiers."

Different camp locations, different military outfits, young men's different perceptions, and older men's memories modified by time can explain the alumni's variety of opinions on the nature of CMTC leaders:

• "I believe the Regular Army officers and sergeants were especially picked and trained for this duty. They were more than 'Boy Scout leaders.' They were very patient and caring and also great teachers." —*Lawrence Doherty.*

CMTC candidates from Michigan in 1930 were inspected for fit after issue of their uniforms on the first day of camp. (Photo from a booklet published by the Military Training Camps Association.)

- "Discipline was identical to that administered to Regular Army recruits." —*C. A. ("Mac") McCaffrey.*
- "Not too hard to recall wonderful treatment by older Regular Army soldiers watching over us like mother hens." —*Gerold Breuer.*
- "The Regular Army NCOs did not like us at all—they had a low regard for our trainees, including the red, white, and blue candidates." —*Russell Eberhardt.*
- "An old Regular Army buck sergeant took one jaundiced look at me and told a corporal (old, too) to 'take this Boy Scout on over to a machine gun company.'" —*James Munday.*
- "Regular Army sergeants and corporals were indeed like Boy Scout leaders to the young CMTC cadets since many kids lied about their ages. The Regular Army NCOs went out of their way to coach, teach and guide those in their charge. The only 'tough' NCOs I recall were those who ran the mess halls." —*Jean Lambert.*

• "The cadre acted like big brothers and yet they taught us well." —*James Cantwell.*

• "I believe the Regular Army sergeants were just as tough on us as they were on regular troops." —*Dave Taylor.*

Two alumni who attended CMTC at the same post, but in different years, had widely contrasting impressions of the regular troops from the Presidio of San Francisco's 30th Infantry Regiment, which was detailed each summer as cadre for the Presidio of Monterey's CMTC. Marco Thorne remembered them this way: "The regulars selected for cadre [1931 through 1935] were more uncles than fathers and treated us like mature people but with a little care. The Army had the attitude that it was responsible for us from the time we left home until we returned into our houses."

Thomas Conrow who trained at Monterey from 1938 to 1939 and at nearby Camp Ord in 1940, had a less sanguine view: "Maybe the 30th Infantry was a tougher outfit than others but they sure weren't Boy Scout types! They were tough, professional soldiers who were drunk a couple days at payday and enjoyed a good fight. They sharpened the edge of the brass buckle on the garrison belt worn with the blouse. Wrap the tongue of the belt around your hand a couple times and you have a potent weapon! The whole 2nd Battalion had a wholesale belt fight the day before we arrived. Lots of bandages."

Evaluations of the quality of CMTC leadership by two contributors depict a balance between firmness and caring that the War Department strived for at all the camps throughout all the years. "We were treated not as recruits of the U.S. Army but as cadets," said Maj. Gen. Eugene Salet who attended at Fort Douglas, Utah, in 1929. "It was recognized that the young men were high school and college students who came from different backgrounds; all were young, impressionable and eager to learn."[6]

"The regular cadre were tough on us, didn't tolerate sissies or homesick boys, but they were understanding and once in a while could be engaged in a friendly dialogue," Robert Fox said of the Fort Benjamin Harrison, Indiana, cadre in the mid-1930s. "The officers were mostly, maybe all, Regular Army, well educated, used good grammar and clean language; I think they were good models for us kids. Most of the noncoms, often with years of service, were strict, didn't stand for any monkey business. They made us feel like, and expected us to be, soldiers."

Abe ("Bud") Rubel, an alumnus of CMTC at Fort McClellan, Alabama, told of a drill instructor who was "like a Boy Scout leader when he had us off to the side." Rubel, who was only 16, confessed to having been among the "two-left-feet" group who were given special instruction by the sergeant. "When the second lieutenant would come over to see how we were doing he [the sergeant] would put on his bad side for the lieutenant."

The permanent cadre, however, wasn't without blemish in their associations with CMTC candidates. Three anecdotes tell of hustling by regular troops—but in each case it appears the instigators weren't necessarily assigned to the CMTC outfit where they were pulling their deals. F. B. McNutt remembered playing blackjack at Fort Monroe with the enlisted cadre, and actually winning—for once.

"At camp end when we were to turn in issue clothing some of the enlisted support cadre (not our company) came to our tents to trade their worn clothing—socks, underwear, etc. for our relatively unused clothing," recalled Eugene Small. "During camp [Camp Dix, 1937] they would try to sell their canteen books (PX chits) for half-price to gain cash until payday."

Joseph Watts, an alumnus of Camp Ord's CMTC, remembered: "We got paid twice while we were there [1939, 1940] but the RAs [Regular Army cadre] from the 3rd Division usually took it from us in games of chance or by selling passes to Monterey or Watsonville. Most of us were 16 or 17 years old and it was our first time away from home—we were easy marks."

Few of the contributors to this book had specific comments

about the leadership provided by their peers—generally referred to as cadet officers and cadet NCOs. Camp yearbooks and newspapers, on the other hand, were replete with digs and inside jokes about the quality, or lack of it, of cadet leaders—but it all seemed to be given and taken in a friendly spirit. The hazing and harassment by upperclassmen so prevalent at military academies and officer candidate schools was never established at CMTC. Perhaps this was because the practice wasn't tolerated by the permanent cadre. Also, proximity has its leveling effect; third- and fourth-year men who were appointed cadet officers or NCOs slept in the same squad tents or barracks as their fellow CMTC troops.

Jack Reeside, however, did remember one cadet leader who fouled up while performing as first sergeant of the day. The reason the event stayed with him through the years is—he was the culprit. "As a test of our leadership abilities, each Blue was periodically assigned the temporary duty as company first sergeant. During my first stint as Top Kick, I moved the company to the mess for lunch. As we neared the mess hall, my mind seemed to go blank and I could not, for the life of me, remember the command to halt. As a result, the company not hearing any command at all marched right through the mess hall doors, which (thank God) were wide open. By the time I did remember the proper command the company had proceeded through the mess hall and was still moving. When I finally stopped the company, I compounded my felony by giving an about face, forward march, and the company went through the mess hall and out the other side."

Memories of disciplinary measures—the little that was ever necessary—reveal that much of the punishment was administered by the candidates themselves. Some of the accounts suggest that the candidate-run "military justice" system took on the characteristics of kangaroo courts. The most often mentioned punishment inflicted by candidates on their erring colleagues was "running the gauntlet." A camp yearbook gave a descriptive definition of the practice: "Running the Gauntlet was a punishment inflicted for negligence in cleanliness and neatness in preparing barracks before inspection. Most of the company, armed with belts, faced each other, while the offenders were forced to run between the lines at the risk of receiving some hard smacks, so that they were not able to sit down the rest of the day with ease."[7]

"The disciplinary action at CMTC [1937 through 1939] was handled more so by the cadets themselves, that is, for minor things," said Bill Bentson, who attended Vancouver Barracks, Washington. "Swiping light bulbs out of tents, walking between stacked rifles, cutting in the chow line, dropping your rifle, not saluting an officer or the colors, disobeying a cadet officer or NCO, the main punishment was the belt line. The whole company would line up with their belt in hand and the offender would have to run through the double line and get belted. This would not be allowed today. It did tend to leave an impression, both physical and mental, on the offender. If you couldn't repeat the general orders for guard duty after a week, this was a belt-line offence."

According to Ray Dearth it was the fecklessness of youth that kept him on the receiving end of military discipline: "At the age of 15 in 1931, I added two years on the application and was accepted for the Basic course in Infantry at Fort Benjamin Harrison. That first year was really a learning experience for me. If there was a wrong way to do something that was me. I did more K.P. than anyone else. I had to run through the belt line because my leggins came unwrapped on our first parade. I even did a punishment walking tour with the full field pack. They would not allow such punishment now but to all of us then it was part of the game and learning process."

The Army's legal authority over these young CMTC civilians appears to have been tenuous at best, but there is no record of any punished candidate complaining to the Inspector General (IG). As a matter of fact, research uncovered no mention of the IG in conjunction with CMTC, and only a few candidates who challenged the disciplinary measures taken against them.

Lawrence Mayland summed up the SOP (Standard Operating Procedure) for CMTC disciplinary actions at most camps: "Breaches of discipline (late from pass, 'mouthing smart,' slow to respond to 'suggestions' et al.) brought swift action in K.P., C.Q. [charge of quarters], even extended guard duty for 'serious infractions.' "

★

Candidates, particularly in the second 10 years of CMTC, encountered many officers from the Organized Reserve Corps (ORC) on two-weeks active duty. Officers from the ORC weren't held in particularly high esteem by those contributing alumni who commented on the performance of reserve officers. In fairness to officers of the ORC assigned to CMTC training, a stingy government and a somnambulant War Department had never allowed the ORC to develop much beyond a paper organization.[8] Opportunities for regular training and professional development were scarce to nonexistent. It is likely, however, that a number of effective reserve officers were assigned to CMTC throughout the years. It's also possible that a young candidate wouldn't have made a strong distinction between a proficient reserve officer and a regular officer, thus retaining no special memory of effective reserve officers.

Marco Thorne's five years of CMTC at Monterey provided him with a keen insight into the relative difference in regular and reserve officers: "During the first two weeks of camp we were supervised by reserve officers assisted by Regular Army enlisted men. It was obvious to us, each year, that the reserve officers were somewhat uncertain of themselves and maybe erred on the side of treating us like kids. The regular enlisted men didn't want to contradict or embarrass their reserve officer superiors and restrained themselves. The reserve officers, after all, in peacetime, were from skeleton, hometown units that had few, if any, enlisted men. We were the annual, short-time exposure to training troops and then only for two weeks. In the last two weeks our officers were the Regular Army officers. Yes, things were different with regular officers. The regular officers were more practiced in supervising young recruits, knew what they were doing, and were firm in what they wanted us to do. The Regular Army enlisted cadre reacted more positively and comfortably to the familiar methods of their own officers. We definitely felt that we were now being treated as grown men."

"The reserve officers changed every two weeks," remembered Robert Wentworth. "Some of them seemed ill at ease, wondering what they were supposed to do."

"As I recall, the reserve officers were probably as green as we were," said Lawrence Doherty.

"The Regular Army cadre of NCOs gave it to us straight so that our military courtesy and discipline for garrison-type duty was standard," recalled William Buning of his training at Fort Screven, Georgia. "The several echelons of reserve officers who were serving their two-week tours [1936–1939] were of easier temperament but interesting as they were just out of ROTC or in business or professions. It gave the training a balanced effect."

At Fort Meade, Maryland, Jack Reeside said the officer cadre consisted entirely of reserve officers. "Many of these officers [1936–1939] were brand-new themselves and often had to resort to training manuals of various types in order to instruct the cadets properly," he said.

Learning experience that it was for many reserve junior officers, the two-weeks duty could provide embarrassing lessons. John Pritchard remembered a young ROTC officer marching the CMTC unit into the side of the mess hall. "Took the Regular Army first sergeant to get us straightened out," he said.

"I recall watching them [reserve officers] practice in the evening and seeing one come to present arms with his sword and piercing his cap on the upstroke," said Thomas Conrow. "The cap just hung there on the sword in mid-air. We wanted to laugh but *no one laughed at an officer!*"

For George Myers, who had four years of Junior ROTC before attending Camp Bullis, Texas, in 1940, a mistake in military etiquette made by a reserve field grade officer left a lasting memory. He told of walking to the drill field with a reserve major. "Like a good ROTC student I walked on his left in step. He informed me in no uncertain terms that I was to walk on his right. 'But sir,' I said, 'the left is where I belong.' After some bitter words, I walked on his right for the remainder of the camp."

William Knolle remembered one reserve company commander at Plattsburg who learned a valuable lesson in leading young summer soldiers and immediately applied it: "The officers we had [1940] for the first two weeks were very professional. Our company won 1st or 2nd place ribbons for each of the semi-weekly reviews. The second group were quite the opposite. The captain carried a small black book and entered any and all infractions. The company did not even place in the first three reviews. The last Saturday in camp we were called to formation where the captain tore up his black book. We then won second place in the last review and the captain left happy."

★ 9 ★

Processing Came First

While training was the prime component of CMTC it wasn't the first event. For most applicants that first event came several weeks or months before reporting to camp. Regulations required that first-year men "undergo a preliminary physical examination by a physician, the results of which must be recorded on the application blank before it is submitted." Inoculations for typhoid fever and smallpox prior to reporting to camp were also required.[1]

To receive the physical free of charge applicants were invited to visit the nearest station where a medical officer of the Regular Army was on duty. If an applicant chose not to use this service he could "at his own expense be examined by any physician but preferably by one who has had military experience."[2] Sometimes the applicant was able to have the physical done for free by a civilian doctor who held a reserve commission, with the doctor earning credit for reserve inactive duty.

Corps commanders were authorized to waive the preliminary physical examination for candidates who were physically qualified at the end of their previous CMTC camp. If the examination was waived, however, those men were required to certify that they were physically fit to undergo the training and hadn't suffered any recent illness.[3] The preliminary physical exam was just that—preliminary. The first order of business for all the candidates when they reached post was lining up for a thorough examination by a Regular Army or Organized Reserve medical doctor. The preliminary examinations, the inoculations, and the on-post physicals left ingrained memories.

Elmer Froewiss had an amusing, if a bit embarrassing, experience with the inoculation procedure: "After being tentatively accepted, one had to have various inoculations. A local doctor would give these, but each individual was sent papers to pick up the serums at an Army installation. I lived in Floral Park, Long Island, New York, at the time [1937] and the nearest base was Mitchel Field. One afternoon I made my way out there and was shown to the lab. As I entered I saw a white-coated medic seated with his feet up on a desk. 'See those glasses over there,' he said, 'Take one of them in that room and fill it up.' Dutifully I picked up what appeared to be an ordinary drinking glass, went in the men's room and filled the glass with tap water. When I handed it back to the medic he said, 'What's this?' 'Water,' I said. 'My God, you didn't drink out of that,' he said, bringing his feet crashing to the floor. When I assured him I hadn't he then asked why I was there. Evidently he thought I had come for a urinalysis. After showing him my papers he gave me my serum and we parted amicably."

"After the application was filled we had to get a physical," Marco Thorne remembered about signing up for CMTC in 1931. "This was arranged with a civilian doctor who might also be in the Army Medical Corps reserve. Doctors kept their commissions during the depression for the money they got if they examined men for CMTC and other purposes.* The doctor I saw scheduled several of us at a time at night and really did not look very hard. Jay Brick, a hometown friend, told me that he used an internationally known Los Angeles psychiatrist who wanted to keep his high rank in the Reserves and who grumbled throughout the physical each time Jay went to him. Needless to say, we had another physical at Monterey on the first day and many were sent home as rejects. Herman [Thorne's brother] was one reject. He

*Medical doctors holding reserve commissions would earn credit for a period of nonactive-duty training, rather than pay. Performing such services helped the doctor retain his reserve commission.

had had a mastoid operation on one ear at age 10 but the civilian doctor passed him. He was rejected at Monterey and the Army gave him his $35 [travel pay] and sent him home."

Harold Bourgoin's examination at Jefferson Barracks, Missouri, was one he never forgot: "A young doctor, a lieutenant, was checking me with his stethoscope and said I had a systolic murmur. I figured my CMTC career was about to have a duration of less than a day; however, the lieutenant asked an elderly lieutenant colonel to check me, saying that he had been 'hearing murmurs all morning.' The colonel checked me and told the lieutenant to clean the wax from his ears."

A detailed description of the physical exam procedure at Camp Knox written by a Medical Corps officer illustrates how well the procedure was organized. Describing the examination stalls the doctor wrote: "The medical officers in each stall then proceeded with the examination of bones, joints, heart, lung and nervous system as well as an examination to determine the presence of *social diseases* [italics added]."[4] This confirmed Fred Featherstone's memory of examinations at Fort Screven, Georgia: "One ritual during the entrance physical which probably shocked some, was the so-called 'short-arm inspection.'"

Soldiers of the 1930s and 1940s built the ritual of "short-arm inspections" to legendary proportions. Few, if any, who soldiered in the 1950s or after ever experienced the notorious formation where the unit was ordered out in the company street clad only in headgear, footwear, and raincoat. Once formed the men were ordered to "skin it back and milk it down" as a medical officer passed each soldier looking for symptoms of venereal disease. Although the legendary formations faded away, the VD examination technique continued, but on an individual basis in the privacy of the doctor's office or the examination stall.*

---

*During my service, which began January 1951, the legendary formations were never observed or heard of except as a practice of the past.

Frank Kreger's memory is probably typical of the sequence of in-processing: "When we arrived at Fort Thomas [1934] we were ushered into the armory where all of our civilian clothes were taken and stored for the period. We had nothing but toilet articles and underclothing left. We were given physical exams, which took part of the morning. Went through the supply line and received our uniforms, which were the old woolen slip-over type [the shirt buttoned down to about midway on the chest] used in World War I. Wraparound puttees and shoes. Overseas type cap, and black tie. That was what we wore for the period, except dungarees when on K.P. Next we received our unit assignments. I was assigned to Co. A (Infantry). Then we were marched to another supply building (shed I should say) and received a bed 'tick,' which we filled with straw for a mattress! Also received pillow, pillow case and two sheets, and two O.D. [olive drab] wool blankets."

A Camp Knox writer, after outlining in some detail the issue process, concluded: "With a loaded barracks bag and all of our civilian belongings thrown across our shoulders, we were taken to our respective barracks. Immediately upon arrival we were requested to divest ourselves of all civilian clothes and don the uniform. Exact fits were one of the marvels of the day. Some short, small guy would have clothing that was made for a tall, stout-built six-footer; a corset-built fellow would have clothing made for a person of huge diameter and vice versa. So you can imagine the comical appearance of the rookie. Exchanges were in vogue for the next few days until each fellow had an appropriate fit. Of all the articles issued, the shoes probably received more comment. Those who were accustomed to wear the 'pin-pointed' shoe that permitted them to foxtrot with becoming grace, found themselves harnessed in a large, heavy, thick-soled, common-sense shoe. After a few days the comment subsided and all of us saw the wisdom of such shoes that enabled us to withstand the marching, hiking, and strenuous army life."[5]

"The biggest shock on arriving at McCoy [Camp McCoy, Wisconsin, 1935]," remembered Gene Schueler, "wasn't the physical but the issuance of World War I heavy woolen uniforms in this seemingly semi-desert area complete with leather puttees."

At least, Schueler wasn't issued the wool wraparound leggings that were issued to most candidates until about 1938. The Army's use of all-wool uniforms for summertime training or combat, and wrap leggings for *any* season or reason defies explanation. The apparent rationale was that wool had a "cooling effect" from the evaporation of all the sweat that it produced. Economy was more likely the reason for inflicting soldiers with what, in 90-degree weather, must have seemed a virtual "hair shirt." The Army was short on money and low on motivation to modernize. Wrap leggings are even harder to rationalize. They were certainly cheaper than leather puttees and probably cost less than the canvas leggings issued in World War II. And since they could only be satisfactorily manipulated by an experienced soldier, they became a status symbol—a point of pride—like being able to roll a perfect cigarette with one hand.

Cecil Roberts, an alumnus of four years of CMTC at Fort Sill, aptly summed up the uniform situation: "Fort Sill in July is no resort! We were issued campaign hats, wool shirts, boot breeches and wrap puttees from World War I. The Regular Army told us the wool shirts and puttees would make us sweat and keep us cooler than cotton uniforms would. I still believe, to this day, that the Army subscribes to the theory: Butt your head against a wall because it feels so good when you stop."[6]

An apt description of the uniform issue was provided by two CMTC alumni. "Our uniforms were leftovers from World War I," remembered Eugene Chase of his training at Fort Crook, Nebraska. "Many of us had trouble keeping the wool wraparound puttees from loosening at the most inopportune times." Henry Grady Young remembered "campaign hats, wool wrap leggings, and of all things, wool shirts. This was the month of July in

Oklahoma [Fort Sill, 1934–1936] with temperature of 95 to 105. We received two changes per week, so by the third day, B.O. was prevalent. The shirts were caked with salt most of the time."

Anyone familiar with the summertime chill at the two Presidios in California will understand why John Moale (who attended the Presidio of San Francisco his first year and Monterey the next) and Thomas Conrow (an alumnus of Monterey's camp in the late 1930s) both described their issued World War I wool clothing, but made no comment about its discomfort.

Fred Moore remembered being issued the chino uniform, which he believed to be its first use, at Fort Benjamin Harrison in 1939. War Department correspondence files appear to confirm Moore's belief, however a 1937 Plattsburg news item mentioned the candidates being supplied chino-khaki clothing, "an innovation in camp regulations."[7]

The chino shirt and trousers would be known for the next 40 years simply as "khakis" even though the color was several shades lighter than the original khaki. Pith helmets were issued at several camps in the late years. Fort Meade, Fort Ethan Allen, and Vancouver Barracks were particularly mentioned by several camp alumni as places where the "Jungle Jim" headgear was issued.

James Duncan was issued canvas leggings at Jefferson Barracks, Missouri. Preferable though they were to wrapped puttees, the hook-together leggings at first gave Duncan a bit of trouble: "I remember [1940] putting on my leggings the wrong way—with the hooks on the inside—and falling while trying to march."

Hanging on to items of issue throughout the month of training and avoiding being charged for the loss of clothing or equipment was sometimes a problem. Marco Thorne recalled the special arrangement that could be made at the Presidio of Monterey to regain lost clothing items: "Laundry was sent twice during the four weeks to Alcatraz Island [in San Francisco Bay, about 115 miles north of Monterey] where the Army had a disciplinary barracks before becoming a federal prison. If one had a shirt or trousers or something missing (we did have sticky fingered candidates), the regulars told us this trick: one put a sack of Bull Durham smoking tobacco or a plug of chewing tobacco in the item of which we wanted back a duplicate. Sure enough, by return sack came a clean duplicate of what we wanted so we could account for all of our clothes when we left camp."

Gaining Momentum

1 9 2 3

The first two years of CMTC were equivalent to a Navy "shakedown cruise" for the War Department, the nine corps areas, and the Army units that conducted the training. By 1923 CMTC had taken on the form it would keep for most of the next 17 years. As mentioned earlier, the minimum age for acceptance was raised in 1922 to 17 years, officially at least. The number of branches offered for training was reduced from nine to six—dropping Air Service, Medical Department, and Motor Transportation Corps. The lessons learned during the two-year shakedown also led to the biggest change and enhancement: the addition of a fourth year of training, adding the Basic course to the Red, White, and Blue courses.

The Secretary of War's figures showed 24,483 men attending the 27 camps conducted in 1923, up from the 22,119 who attended 28 camps in 1922.[1] By the end of July 34,500 young men had applied, including John Coolidge (the not-quite 17-year-old son of Vice President Calvin Coolidge), who had signed up for the Camp Devens CMTC.[2]

Candidate Coolidge would suddenly become even more prominent shortly after his Devens training began, when he became known as "President Coolidge's son John" as a result of the unexpected death of President Harding in San Francisco on Tuesday, August 2. Citizens' Military Training Camps, joining a mourning nation, conducted solemn memorial services.

Donald Armstrong, who at age 16 attended the August CMTC

at Plattsburg (one also was conducted in July), recalled the President's death occurring shortly after the camp started. He also remembered that the residents of his squad tent were "representative of CMTC as a whole. We had a farm boy from Delaware and two lads from the tough section of Newark, New Jersey, and one who had just completed his first year at Yale and one or two more and myself. The Yaley was really the sophisticate of the whole group. He could tell us what really made the world go round."

At Devens, young Coolidge, now under closer scrutiny by camp officials and the press (but no Secret Service contingent in those placid days), was making a good account of himself. The *New York Times* reported "John Coolidge, son of President Coolidge, was among those scoring high [on the rifle range], with a total of 43 out of a possible 50."[3]

That summer a vaudeville circuit was formed to play in moving picture theaters at 25 Army posts. The Army now operated more than 100 movie theaters in the nine corps areas and the Hawaii Department.[4] Some of the "picture shows" that candidates might have viewed that summer were *Blood and Sand* with Valentino, the comedy *Grandma's Boy* with Harold Lloyd, and *Oliver Twist* starring Jackie Coogan, all released in 1922. And perhaps some saw the current *Little Old New York* with Marion Davies, *Rosita* starring Mary Pickford, and *The Hunchback of Notre Dame* with Lon Chaney, Sr.

The movies were still silent, but for those post theaters boasting a piano or organ—and with someone who could play the instrument—the audience might have heard 1922's hit "Chicago, That Toddling Town," and even "followed the bouncing ball" while singing along to "My Buddy," also published in 1922.

For company buglers and Army band cornet or trumpet players who aspired to emulate some of the nation's top jazz players, 1922 and 1923 were good years. Henry Busse's "Hot Lips," published in 1922, was followed in 1923 by Clarence Williams' "Sugar

Blues," which carried Clyde McCoy to national fame, and made the Harmon "Waa-waa" mute required equipment for the *compleat cornetist*. For those players who preferred the open bell, the upbeat "Bugle Call Rag" also came out in 1923.

The all-black review *Runnin' Wild* introduced the Charleston, a dance that took the nation by storm, adding heat to the young folks the country was already calling "Flaming Youth." CMTC candidates who were inclined to take a whirl on the dance floor and hadn't already learned the Charleston's steps might have had a chance to pick it up at the service clubs' weekend dances that summer.

The negative impact of Prohibition was becoming increasingly apparent. At least 5,000 speakeasies were reported to be operating in New York City alone. CMTC wouldn't escape the blight created by the national law. In July the mayor of Wrightstown, New Jersey, just outside Camp Dix, warned "camp followers," including bootleggers, to leave town immediately.[5] In another article, the *New York Times* reported that the New Jersey merchants of illicit booze had been chased off by the local Ku Klux Klan. The *Times* editorialized: "No matter what happened to them, no sympathy would have been deserved by criminals who sold intoxicants to the young men [CMTC candidates] preparing themselves for exercising the highest duty of citizenship, but harmful indeed would have been the establishment of the seeming precedent that only by lynchers [the KKK] can certain evils be abolished."[6]

Throughout CMTC's history many national organizations and their local chapters were generous in their support of the program, and the Army was more than happy to accept their efforts. However, the KKK certainly was not among the organizations whose support the Army solicited or desired.

Typical of the enthusiastic support given CMTC by prominent organizations was the "Rotary Clubs Day" at Plattsburg on the final Saturday of the August 1923 camp. More than 100 Rotarians from throughout the state were feted to a review by 2,000

John Coolidge as he enrolled in CMTC at Camp Devens, Massachusetts. After beginning CMTC in 1923 the Vice President's son suddenly became the son of President Coolidge. (Photo courtesy of National Archives.)

candidates and a later demonstration of the "new athletic test known as National Yardstick," as well as a 12-mile relay race involving 1,200 of the student soldiers. The Rotarians, in turn, presented the CMTC regiment with a stand of organizational colors.[7] Two days later, on Monday, the Plattsburg CMTC troops fell out for a special review for New York Governor Alfred E. Smith, where "the largest crowd of the Summer thronged the parade ground."[8]

In late July the president of the New York Stock Exchange, Raymond L. Cromwell, in conjunction with the Boys' Work

Financial District YMCA was the host at a luncheon given for the young men working on Wall Street who would soon be departing for CMTC training. One of the speakers was Grenville Clark, a distinguished—but little known nationally—pioneer of the Plattsburg Movement and the MTCA.[9]

As supportive of CMTC as civic, veteran, and other organizations were, none could match the unbelievable support given by the "Gray Old Lady," the prestigious *New York Times*. The day after John Coolidge's excellent showing on the rifle range at Camp Devens was reported, the *Times* noted on page two that Candidate Thomas M. Stranney of Brooklyn had fired the first perfect score on the rifle range at the Plattsburg CMTC.[10]

The front page of the Sunday, August 26, edition, in a two column story carried a headline reading:

NINE STUDENT SOLDIERS OUTWIT REGULARS,
GET PAST CRACK ARMY BRIGADE AT CAMP DIX[11]

(Earlier that month on page 24, the *Times* carried a three-inch story about a riot in Munich, Germany, on August 14 started by the Hitler Nationalists.)[12]

It might have better suited the War Department if some of CMTC reportage had gone unprinted. The July 28 issue carried the headline "Color Line at Camp" over a story reporting that the NAACP (National Association for the Advancement of Colored People) had written Secretary of War Weeks protesting the rejection of the CMTC application of Anthony R. Mayo, Jr. of Bloomsfield, New Jersey, because of color.[13] How Secretary Weeks responded isn't known; nevertheless, CMTC training would continue to be denied young black men until the mid-1930s and then was offered only at segregated camps in three locations.

That summer a feature story appeared about "two girl pals," Aletta Carey and Percy Paine, from Charles City, Iowa, who wrote the President asking the government to establish a CMTC for females

General of the Armies Pershing posed in 1919 with his staff on the steps of the State, War, and Navy Building in Washington, D.C. Although the identities of the other officers are not available, the officer standing fourth from the left is George C. Marshall, Pershing's aide-de-camp. (National Archives.)

where "real training, as shooting, drills and everything, similar to the boys," would be conducted. Asked for a response the Adjutant General's office issued a statement saying the letter raised "some most important questions which . . . will be carefully studied."[14]

Although the response might have seemed (and even been) disingenuous, in August 1921 Chief of Staff Pershing, commenting about the number of physical defects found during the Would War I draft, had stated "the nation would gain if the [CMTC] courses were made compulsory for every boy and *girl* [emphasis added]."[15] It would take another World War, however, to cause the government to inaugurate military training for women.

The physical state of the nation's youth remained a subject of concern to the government. The War Department released a report that said the first two years of CMTC had confirmed what was found during the late war (World War I) that 5 to 6 out of every 10 young men suffered from "more or less serious physical defects." In 1922 4.1 percent of 23,000 men examined were rejected and 470 of every 1,000 had defects that hampered them in their training. In the first two weeks of training, however, the report stated that improvements in the physical defects were noted. The Army considered that the young men attending CMTC had been "loaned to the country by their parents," causing "extraordinary precautions" to be taken. The report also claimed that candidates received treatment for medical problems that would never have brought them to a doctor in civilian life.[16]

An item in the report was indicative of the economic and health deprivations that still existed in the south. In 1922 at Fourth Corps Area's Camp McClellan, Alabama, 20 percent of the CMTC applicants showed hookworm infection. Fourth Corps Area officials took positive action in 1923 and organized a "Special Training Company." The company was made up of 130 men who were evaluated as physically unfit to meet regular training requirements at the time of enrollment. At the end of three weeks, 127 of the candidates had gained an average of 13 pounds per man. The final average for the group in the physical efficiency test was only three points below that obtained by the regular CMTC men. In 1924 the Army endorsed the idea of special training camps and authorized each corps area to adopt the plan as it saw fit.[17]

"Extraordinary precautions" or not, the Army couldn't be everywhere at once. An off-duty weekend boating accident in Lake Champlain involved four Plattsburg candidates. "Plattsburg

Hero Saves Two Buddies, One Youth Drowns," read the *Times* headline over a story of the accidental drowning of 17-year-old Albert W. Kampman of Jersey City, and the heroic actions of another CMTC candidate, William B. Tremble, 18, who swam two miles through the stormy lake to go for help for his two fellow survivors.[18]

CMTC was making news—good, tragic, and controversial—and in three years had reached a definite prominence.

Traveling to Camp

For many young men who had signed up for CMTC, the first big adventure was getting to camp. Some of the most vivid reminiscences by the contributors to this book were their stories of that travel. Poignant, amusing, unusual, even unbelievable—these anecdotes bring to life the youthful enthusiasms, naïveté, and guts of these summertime soldiers.

CMTC travel regulations as set forth by the War Department certainly held out no promise of high adventure. Straightforward and uncompromising were these rules of the road, as can be seen from the following:

Transportation to camp is furnished under the following conditions:
(1) The applicant may pay his own way to camp and be reimbursed after arrival there at the rate of 5 cents per mile over the shortest usually traveled route between his home and camp; or
(2) He may apply for a Government transportation request or railway ticket, and upon arrival at camp be paid 1 cent per mile for the distance actually traveled to cover cost of meals en route.

If the applicant selects method (2) above, he must use the Government transportation request, or railway ticket, for under no circumstances will he be entitled to receive 5 cents per mile.
(3) No candidate discharged from camp for misconduct or his own convenience will be paid the 5 cents per mile travel allowance; instead, he will be furnished a Government transportation request from the camp to his home and 1 cent a mile for subsistence.[1]

In the early 1920s the most common means of transportation to CMTC was by rail. In 1923 hundreds of lads emerged from a special train at the Camp Knox station. Billed caps, white shirts, jackets, and neckties obviously were de rigueur *for young men of the time. (Photo from the 1923 CMTC yearbook,* The Mess Kit.*)*

These dry paragraphs give no clue to the multitude of travel methods conceived and practiced by the youth of the era.

None was more adventurous than a free, but hazardous method—riding the rails. Three CMTC alumni recalled their experiences traveling in box cars—an illegal mode of travel made popular, and sometimes necessary, by the conditions of the time. Russell Haag, who first attended CMTC in 1935 at the Presidio of Monterey, had his freight-hopping experience the year before he attended his first camp. However, without his brave and desperate act, motivated by the Great Depression, Haag would have been unlikely to have attended CMTC or ever to have accomplished what he did in his life.

"I left home from a farm in Eden Valley, Minnesota, in 1934

when I was 17 years old. Rode freight trains to Sacramento, California, where I applied for Camp Carlton, a camp in Redwood City [about 25 miles south of San Francisco] for homeless boys during the Depression. On my way to California I worked in the harvest fields in North Dakota for 25 cents an hour. I was at Camp Carlton for about a month when Colonel Kelly, owner of the Palo Alto Military Academy, selected me to work at the academy as a handy man. I worked my way through Palo Alto High School, Menlo School and Junior College, and Stanford University with the help of some wonderful people." Haag said the band master at the academy suggested he attend CMTC. By then he was able to make the relatively short trip to Monterey by more conventional and safer means. After two years of CMTC it was on to Stanford and a Navy commission. Haag retired as a lieutenant commander and afterward ran a successful real estate business in Palo Alto.

The travel memories of Archie Stewart, an alumnus of the 1936 camp at Fort Sill, Oklahoma, also are indicative of the hard times in the 1930s: "In 1936, I was a 14-year-old high school boy in Commerce, Texas, with a newspaper route that was nearly five-miles long with over 100 newspapers to deliver each morning. I found out I could join the National Guard, drill one night a week, be furnished shoes (to take home and shine and walk my paper route in) and be furnished a wool shirt (which I could take home and have cleaned and pressed—to keep warm on paper route), get paid $1.00 for each drill, and only have to hitchhike 16 miles over to Greenville. Then the Cotton Belt (Freight) Lines furnished free transportation back to Commerce at 11 P.M. In addition I found out that I could go to CMTC at Fort Sill and they would pay me mileage to and from, which would amount to about $30 for 30 days. I and several others hitchhiked and rode freight trains to Oklahoma for the training. I was 'discharged' after about two or three weeks because they found out that I was in the National Guard (had to go to guard camp), but they paid me the travel anyway.

Russell Haag on one of several freight trains that brought him from his home in Minnesota to Palo Alto, California, in the depth of the Great Depression. The next year he attended the 1935 CMTC at the Presidio of Monterey. This dangerous and illegal—but economical—means of transportation also was used by two other CMTC alumni whose memories are quoted here. (Photo courtesy of Russell Haag.)

. . . When we rode the freight train from Fort Worth to Fort Sill we were thrown off the train at Wareka, Oklahoma, and told to hit the highway for the other 20 to 30 miles, which we did."

Just as Russell Haag had, Eugene Salet began life on his own at an early age. About 1924, at age 13, he left his family's ranch to escape his abusive stepfather and rode his horse the 15 miles to Lovelock, Nevada, the nearest town. "I lived alone throughout my high school days," Salet said, "and by the grace of God, and the fact that I was a fairly good athlete and was blessed with an understanding young coach, I survived some very difficult times."

In 1929, 18-year-old Salet decided to attend CMTC at Fort Douglas, Utah. It seemed to him that the only feasible way to travel the 500 miles to Salt Lake City was by hopping a freight. So one afternoon he vaulted into an empty boxcar of a Southern Pacific freight train moving slowly through Lovelock:[2] "As my eyes penetrated the gloom inside of the car, I learned that I wasn't alone. Huddled in the dark corner of the car was a slight figure that I first assumed to be a young boy. I said, 'Hello, how are you?' but the person made no answer. Looking closer I noted that the person was a young female. Again I said, 'Hello,' and this time she responded with a fairly weak 'Hello.' I sat down alongside her and struck up a conversation. I asked her where she was going and what she was doing riding a freight train. At first she was quite wary of me, but then she apparently noticed that I was no older that she, and she began to loosen up and talk. The young woman was on her way to Salt Lake City. She had left home in search of work. Her father had abandoned the family, and her mother, with five other children, was struggling to make ends meet. I accepted her story at face value—it wasn't too different from mine. I asked her if she wasn't concerned about traveling by herself in a male environment. She said yes but that she thought the freight was a better way to get to her destination than to hitchhike."

Hunger setting in later that night, Salet reached into his dufflebag for sandwiches he had brought along and offered one to the young woman: "She literally devoured it. I asked her when she had last eaten. She said the day before. I also had a canteen of water in my duffel bag, and I passed that to her; she drank from it thirstily and gratefully. I gave her another sandwich and took one myself. I asked the girl if she had any money. She indicated that she had a few dollars but beyond that she had no prospects of further funds until she found work. She said if she didn't find work immediately upon arriving in Salt Lake City that she might well have to resort to, and I quote her, 'selling my body.' I asked her if she meant by that (I wasn't the most worldly guy in the world) that she intended to become a 'hooker.' She asked what a hooker was. I told her a hooker was a woman who worked the streets 'selling her body'—a whore. She said she had no intention of becoming a whore and hoped that she wouldn't have to 'sell my body'—she insisted on using that saying which was to me a quaint expression. I now began to act like a 'father confessor' with all of my worldly wisdom, which wasn't a lot.

"She was grateful for the food and water and much to my amazement she asked if I expected payment. I reminded her that she had just told me she had little money. She said that if I expected payment she would have to pay me by 'the use of my body.' I damn near fell out of the boxcar. Again I assumed the role of father confessor. With all of the 'worldly experience' at my command, I told her that she should be very careful of how she approached this possible new profession because of the many pitfalls involved. I also told her that she should have stayed in the state of Nevada and entered a whorehouse for basic training if she was going to take on the world's oldest profession as a means of livelihood.

"She asked me how I knew all of this. I told her while I hadn't learned this by 'on the job training,' I had learned it from my dear friend, the Madam, the generalissimo of the bullpens in Lovelock. I told her the story of my ice deliveries to this restricted area, how the operation was carefully controlled, and what a dear and close friend I had in Mrs. Graham [the Madam]. I felt my worldly expertise was about exhausted and decided that I would curl up and try to take a nap. I suggested that she do the same thing, and we both were soon sleeping away, curled up on the hard floor of the boxcar. We arrived [the next morning in Salt Lake City] in the huge S.P. rail yards shortly after daylight. The railroad yards were alive with railroad bulls [railroad detectives]. I took my female 'hobo' in charge and we managed to find our way out of the railroad yard and onto a main street leading into the center of Salt Lake City. Here I bid my boxcar companion goodbye. She gave me a quick hug, turned, and marched resolutely down the street."

Many others also chose rail travel, it being the country's principal means of transportation at the time. Although it was a far less adventurous way to travel, being a legitimate, paying passenger still provided some lasting memories. Elmer Froewiss, who grew up in the New York City area, remembered anxiously awaiting orders as an alternate applicant to the 1937 Camp Dix CMTC: "We [a group of alternates] all knew which day we were to leave for camp and had been told to watch for our orders and tickets. Well, when the day came I had no orders, and I was a pretty downhearted boy. I moped around the house all morning and after lunch my mother gave me a scarce quarter to go to the movies, it being a Saturday. The movies were 10 cents and for 15 cents I could buy a quarter-pound of milk chocolate 'broken-bars.' These were huge chunks of chocolate about an inch and a half thick that were sold in bulk. I guess that is the reason my blood sugar runs high to this day, but then it was just the thing to salve my broken heart. When I returned from the movies the atmosphere around the house was electric, and my mother, sisters, and brother were all wearing what I would later learn were 'shit-eating' grins. The telegram had come, and I was to report to the Pennsylvania Station in New York City on Monday morning. Needless to say my mood changed completely, and I walked the clouds the mile or so back to the Long Island Railroad Station to check on the train schedule for Monday morning. The station was closed, but at the end of the platform two men were in a small shed from which they operated the crossing gates. I told them my tale, and of course they had a schedule. As I turned to leave, one of them said, 'Son, if you're going into the military, let me give you some advice. Always keep your mouth shut and your bowels open, and you'll get along all right.' I always remembered that, and found it a pretty good axiom."

Some remember taking troop trains out of New York City to Plattsburg or Dix: "Getting on a troop train in Penn Station with hundreds of New York City 'street-wise' youths was an experience for us that better prepared us for life," said Arthur Dorie of his trip to Fort Dix in 1940.

Maxwell Hamilton remembered his trip this way: "And so,

barely making the minimum age of 17, and about as raw and gangly as it was possible to be, McGovern [his buddy] and I were among almost the first of the New York City contingent to arrive at Grand Central Station the following July 1, [1927] to board the special 13-car train that was to take us the approximately 300 miles northward to Plattsburgh [*sic*]."[3]

It is reasonably certain that none of the former CMTC candidates who contributed to this account were among the approximately 40 CMTC applicants who left Pittsburgh Wednesday, July 5, 1939, on a Baltimore and Ohio Railroad train headed for Fort George G. Meade.[4] Had the rail journey occurred later in the 20th century the participants might have immortalized the experience as "The Train Ride from Hell." Arriving at Fort Meade at 7:06 A.M. the next morning four of the train's five passenger cars were in various states of wreckage. Fire extinguishers were missing, 38 light bulbs were broken or missing, one entire coach seat was gone and two seat backs couldn't be found, men's restrooms were trashed—to name just part of the damage list presented to camp officials by the railroad. Including labor, the railroad company estimated the damage at $238.17. An examination of the detailed list shows the replacement cost for the 38 light bulbs amounted to only $6.60, indicating that the total damage would have amounted to thousands of dollars at current prices.

Army officials started an immediate investigation and on July 13 convened a three-officer board of inquiry. Forty-four men were interviewed under oath; evidently all the CMTC-bound passengers. The group, who were from Pittsburgh and surrounding communities, consisted of first-, second-, and third-year men. The testimony showed a general reluctance to "squeal" on colleagues and amazingly short memories for such young men. Some saw unidentified men drinking something from a bottle, but no one admitted having a bottle of whiskey much less taking a drink from one. The main suspect appeared to be a first-year applicant who earned the nickname, "The Mad

Russian" (a popular comic character on "The Eddie Cantor" radio show), from the pajama top he was wearing, which he admitted to the board "was a flashy one. Red and black."[5]

The board adjourned four days later and in its report found that "The Mad Russian" and two others, a Basic candidate and a White, plus a fourth young man who had failed his entrance physical and departed, were the principal culprits. The three were dismissed from camp and barred from future CMTC attendance. The board also found that since the men were traveling in a civilian status neither the U.S. government "nor any of its agents are in any way responsible for the loss" to the railroad. The board concluded: "The Baltimore & Ohio railroad could have avoided all damage had proper police precautions been taken. *The past experiences of this type* [of] *passenger should have warned them of possible damage* [emphasis added]."[6]*

Howard ("Dusty") Rhodes, who grew up in the Canal Zone, covered many hundreds of miles on water before he and a group of buddies reached a troop train departing from New York: "Five of us 'Zonians,' all of us June 1940 graduates of Balboa High School, attended the Plattsburg camp that year. Our mode of travel to New York City was by Panama Canal Company steamer. We paid our own round trip expenses from Balboa, Canal Zone, to New York where we rode a troop train to Plattsburg." The *New York Times* devoted five paragraphs to their long voyage.[7]

Ralph Hofmann, who attended CMTC at Fort Meade in 1937, also took a water route, although shorter: "During the 1930s steamships made overnight runs between the Virginia peninsula area (Norfolk and Fort Monroe) to Washington and Baltimore. Most of us going to Fort Meade from the peninsula went both ways by those steamers."

---

*Research for this book turned up no other instances of vandalism or blatant misconduct by CMTC candidates. It would be unrealistic, however, to believe that, during the program's 20 years, there were not other occurrences of collective and destructive rowdyism by candidates.

"We went there on the train," recalled Mark Eastin of the first trip to Camp Knox in 1921 made by him and several other candidates from Union County in western Kentucky. "Those were the days before good roads. We had to go from Sturgis up to Henderson [both in Kentucky] and change trains there to the L.H. and St. Louis to Louisville. Then we hired hacks—they were Reo cars—to take us down to Camp Knox."

Roads were steadily improving during the 1920s, however, and by 1924 when Eastin attended his fourth year of CMTC at Knox—this time as an acting officer—he traveled there in his sporty roadster.

That same year another candidate headed for camp by auto: "Bill Bulow made the trip from home, several states away, via a Lizzie. He claims the trip was a money-making proposition as Henry [both Lizzie and Henry were among the nicknames for the Model-T Ford] doesn't need much gas."[8]

Candidates who traveled by automobile from 1926 on were more than likely to be entertained with roadside advertisements for a brushless shaving cream that became a national institution. Spaced about 100-yards apart on the right side of the highway would appear doggerel such as: "Every Shaver / Now Can Snore / Six More Minutes / Than Before / By Using / BURMA SHAVE"— or "Does Your Husband / Misbehave / Grunt and Grumble / Rant and Rave? / Shoot the Brute Some / BURMA SHAVE."[9]

The *New York Times* reported a variety of transportation means to Plattsburg employed by some trainees in 1926. Two New Jersey lads, Alexander Hutz of Fairview and Albert Simonette of Union City, covered the more than 400 miles to Plattsburg on bicycles, camping "by wayside on the way." The *Times* reported "28 machines, mostly flivvers, gayly marked with the names and destination of the owners and occupants" parked at the end of the company street. No candidate was more adventurous than Clinton Murray, an 18-year-old high school student from Rome, New

York, who "arrived in camp this morning after having walked from his home to Plattsburg, a distance of nearly 300 miles."[10] In 1935 Arnold Leroy Bolton hitchhiked 1,000 miles from Wisconsin back to his home state of New York to report to CMTC at Madison Barracks.[11]

An Ohio lad named Riley Miner assigned to Signal Co. at Camp Knox in 1925, also had a fascinating trip:[12] "Some come by train, some come by Fords and some bum it through. Try the latter and you sure get some thrills. Bumming is not what it's cracked up to be but it is the best way to get anywhere when you are broke.

"Finishing with high school at Canton, Ohio, this year . . . I decided to roll my pack and hit the highway for the good old camp.

"A young chap [a Dane] came along in an old Ford touring [car]. He was headed for the wheat fields in Kansas to work during the harvest. . . . It was great to hear some of the stories he told about the army in the 'Old Country' and about his experiences along the trip. I rode to Columbus, Ohio, with him that afternoon and stayed at my aunt's for a couple of days. . . .

"[Later] I got a lift into Springfield. I stopped there to see some friends on the *Springfield News*. Between Springfield and Dayton I had . . . to walk about 20 miles with a 35 pound pack that seemed to get 10 pounds heavier every step I took.

"Almost into Dayton a traveling salesman picked me up and took me to Cincinnati. That night I stayed at the National Guard Armory there after having to get permission from nearly everyone from a 'shavetail' to a colonel. The trouble with Cincinnati is that no one knows anything about the place.

"From Covington [Kentucky], which is just across the river from Cincinnati, I took the Dixie Highway on the way to Lexington.

"I don't believe that I have ever seen so many twists and turns and up and down grades in my life as there were on that road. The road followed the tops of hills and the view was wonderful; the atmosphere was very clear and one could see for miles just like an aeroplane ride. Caught several lifts en route but had to stay along the road that night in my pup tent only a few miles from Lexington. . . .

"It was great there by myself until about three in the morning when a storm came up and, not having driven the stakes deep enough, the wind blew it [the tent] down on top of me. Some job trying to put up a pup tent in a strong wind all by your lonesome and the rain coming down in sheets.

"About noon the next day, bedraggled and wet, I reached Lexington. I went to the Troop 'C' Saddle Club where I dried my blankets and stuff out, staying in their drill hall that night. They sure treat a fellow royal. They gave me a good bed and good chow. I helped the caretakers exercise the horses the next day. I stayed there for two days. . . .

"I wanted to see the capital of Kentucky, so reluctantly started on my way again. Was hardly out of Lexington when a state senator picked me up and took me the whole way to Frankfort, the capital.

"The next and last stopping place was Louisville. I couldn't imagine a street being so long as Seventh Avenue [leading south to Camp Knox] was that night. . . . [After] walking for three hours . . . I got to the city limits. I sure was ready to hit the hard cold ground that night.

"By noon the 25th of June I finally arrived at Camp Knox. . . .

"Tired but happy and glad to hear Taps blow once again, I turned in that night, hoping never again to take that long bumming trip."

★ I2 ★

Being Paid and Heading Home

The five-cent-a-mile pay offered by the CMTC program occupied a big place in the memories of many of the CMTC alumni. Jack Reeside, who attended Fort Meade from 1936 through 1939, said: "As I was at that period living in Hyattsville, Maryland, which was approximately 21 miles from the post, I received the enormous sum of $1.50. This would be a pittance today, but in my young inexperienced mind, it seem like a fortune. Remember, these were Depression years. I have always strongly suspected that many of my fellow cadets were more interested in the travel pay awarded than in patriotism."

Chester Carpenter agreed: "In 1937 some people actually went to CMTC for the money involved. They paid nothing, of course, but they took care of expenses. I think my total pay from Canastota, New York, to Plattsburg was $14 or $15."

"In that first year, 1935, the depression had not yet reached its end for my family," said Fred Featherstone, who attended Fort Screven, Georgia, for four years. "The $61 in travel pay was a lot of money for me at that time."

"Some smarter cadets got on to this five cents a mile we were paid for travelling to camp," Bill Bentson recalled. "They may have only lived 20 miles from the camp, so if they had a relative who lived say 400 miles from the camp, they would use their relative's address, when registering for camp. This would give them $20 in place of $1 and on a round trip they would have $40 and that was more than a Regular Army corporal was paid for a month."

Robert Sumner, who lived in Portland, Oregon, and attended Vancouver Barracks, remembered "pay call": "During the first week of training, we lined up to sign the payroll and I collected my 50 cents. In the last day or so, we were paid our return fare—another 50 cents in my case."

Daniel Hughes, who lived in Sault Sainte Marie, Michigan, remembered: "I lived about one mile from camp [Fort Brady] so I received my pay of five cents in a large envelope, which I immediately spent on a bottle of pop in the PX."

Southern Californian Tom Conrow provided an account that would indicate that it wasn't just the candidates who sometimes "played games" with the travel regulations. The Army, or at least the Ninth Corps Area headquarters, also was known to have manipulated the rules in the Army's favor. "If some towns had no applications, the space was used for someone else," he said. Even though Conrow was due travel pay from Ontario in Southern California, his first year he was paid from some town in California's San Joaquin Valley, much closer to Monterey. "After Basic, though, I always got a nice pay from Ontario."

With about $50 of travel money in hand, Eugene Salet could have purchased a ticket back to Lovelock, Nevada, but he said, "I concluded that I would be foolish to spend funds in this manner, so I found my way to my port of entry in Salt Lake City—the Southern Pacific railroad yard." This time he had no female travel mate, but he was almost caught by a "bull" in Nevada.

Even late in life David Gray was still admonishing himself about the manner in which he headed for home from Camp Knox: "My father worked for the C. and I.E. Railroad and as such got me a round-trip pass to Knox. Our last day in camp we were issued sufficient money to pay our rail fare home. We got the money at one table and were then supposed to go to another table and buy our ticket from a RR agent, but I slipped out through a side window. That evening our company clerk got a little tipsy and I talked him into giving me my discharge certificate. I then caught a late train and arrived home the next morning. Tony [his friend with whom he had traveled to Camp Knox] told me later that they looked all over for me the next morning. I've done some stupid things in my life and this was one of them. I could have easily cashed the RR ticket in when I got home. I missed the opportunity to say goodbye to the many friends I had made and I spent a miserable night all told. The Illinois Central dumped me off in the small Kentucky town of Princeton where I spent about four hours waiting for a train to Evansville. The place was completely shut down, not even a stray dog around. And it was chilly. Technically since I had my papers I was discharged but in my own mind I was AWOL."

Donald Martin's return from CMTC was truly unforgettable: "I was returning home from Fort Hancock [1938] with a suitcase full of dirty clothes. The Army boat dropped us at the Battery in New York. I then took a subway to midtown to catch the Long Island Railroad train home. The suitcase was one of those very long ones that they used during Prohibition to carry liquor in but I didn't think anything about the unusual length that was soon to cause me much trouble and embarrassment.

"I changed subway trains at an unattended station where the exit turnstiles were composed of iron bars about three inches apart and arranged in the usual cruciform shape. The turnstile extended from the station floor to ceiling as did the fence in which the turnstile was placed. I was one of the first off of the train and I charged into the turnstile with my long suitcase not realizing that it wouldn't fit until the revolving turnstile came to a screeching halt with me and my suitcase partially inside; I couldn't go forward, I couldn't go back. There was no guard to release me. I was trapped like a monkey in a cage.

"Meanwhile the passengers behind me were clamoring to get on their way. The only other turnstile was at the opposite end of the station. To make things worse, another train came in and disgorged its passengers. The jeering of the irate commuters was getting to me. I decided to climb up on the suitcase to see if I could break it loose. I jumped up and down on it till it finally broke with a loud pop, dumping my clothes all over the pavement. I was finally able to get through the turnstile followed by the mob who trampled all over my clothes, even kicking some of them a considerable distance away. Today, I would probably leave them there, but times were hard in those days so I had to retrieve the clothes, tying them in bundles as the suitcase was a complete loss. So ended my 1938 CMTC at Fort Hancock."

Then there is Elmer Froewiss' tale of his trip home from Camp Dix in 1937, on a troop train headed for New York: "The train to New York City naturally had quite a few cars to accommodate the large numbers of us going that way. I mention that as it adds a bit to the incident that I'm about to describe. When settled on the train, and after it had gone some miles, box lunches were passed out, and almost immediately the word was passed through the train 'Don't eat your apple.' I didn't know why this was but I soon found out.

"Eventually we stopped at a station in New Jersey to let some of the fellows off. I don't know which town it was, but the tracks were elevated above what appeared to be the main part of town, and the main street ran under them at about a 75-degree angle just north of the station platform. As the train departed, seemingly on cue all the windows and doors on the platform side of the train were flung open, and as each car cleared the station everyone heaved his apple with full force into the street below. As my car passed over the street I did the same, and looking down I could see hundreds of apples in the street. I don't recall seeing any people, and I'm sure that if there were any on the street to begin with they soon ducked indoors. All of this was done with great glee, and it seems to me now that by default or design those with the best throwing arms were allotted the best throwing positions on the doorways of the train.

"I've thought about this incident many times over the years, usually with some degree of guilt. What must the townspeople have thought about this, when all of a sudden they were bombarded with hundreds of apples? Was this a yearly ritual, which they knew was coming? It seems to me that the way the whole thing came about it must have been a regular part of the trip home. Though most of us on the train were first-timers, there was a good proportion of second- and third-year men on the train. But if it happened every year, didn't the people complain to the Army, or at least to the railroad? The Army could have put MPs on the train to stop it. Maybe the townspeople liked getting those apples. At the end of World War II I made almost weekly train trips between Washington and New York for six months, and on each trip I'd try to figure out which station it was. The best I ever came up with was Metuchen, New Jersey, but I was never sure about it."

Is it possible that some old-timers in Metuchen, or some other New Jersey town, still recount the legend of the "Annual Summertime Apple Attack" of the 1930s?

★ 13 ★

"A Growing Institution"

1924–1925

The demand during the past fiscal year was so great and so insistent that no doubt remains as to the acceptance of the camps by the country as a national institution of great value. They are naturally a growing institution, of worth in peace as well as for war." So wrote the Secretary of War in his annual report for fiscal year 1924 (July 1, 1923 to June 30, 1924), during which most of the 1923 camps were held.[1]

The public's favorable exposure to CMTC and its growing popularity among young American males began to persuade Congress—severely parsimonious during the 1920s in matters concerning the military—to steadily increase its annual CMTC appropriation. Applications for the 1924 camps numbered about 50,000, and there was enough money to train more than 32,000 candidates—an increase of about 8,000 from a year before—at 28 camps.[2]

Maj. Gen. Robert C. Davis, Adjutant General, reported attendance statistics for 1924: "Wide geographical distribution has been a guiding principle in arranging attendance. Applications were received in 1924 from all but 247 of the 3,089 counties in the United States [almost 93 percent of the nation's counties], and actual enrollments were secured from all but 420 counties. On the basis of the estimated total population of the United States, the rate of C.M.T.C. enrollment in 1924 was 1 to 3,255 inhabitants."[3]

General Pershing, whose retirement as chief of staff had been

announced for mid-September, demonstrated his continued dedi-
cation to CMTC on a three-week farewell tour of installations
around the country that were engaged in CMTC or National
Guard training.[4] Pershing's visit to Camp Knox was one of Mark
Eastin's keenest CMTC memories: "They had a review, and it was
pretty good for a bunch of kids that went up there just for a month.
So here's what several of us did: We knew that the general was
going to the officers' club for a reception after the review. So about
15 or 20 of us took off to go over there [near the officers' club].
[As Pershing and his party departed the post] we knew what lane
he was going out to get to the main highway. We stationed
ourselves about 50 yards apart—just one person—all the way back
to the officers' club. When his entourage came by, we'd each give
and get a separate salute. And some of the boys on the end said
Pershing and his group were catching on. They were all laughing
as they kept passing us. But they gave us full returns of our salutes
and we thought that was great."

The retiring chief of staff's tour also provided Harry Traffert
with a memory he would never forget. He said he was in the
Cavalry troop that passed in review at the ceremony for Pershing
at Fort Des Moines, Iowa: "My horse ran away with me on the
way back to the stables and I was the butt of many jokes for my
horsemanship."

★

Donald Armstrong, who attended five training camps in the
four summers between 1923 and 1926 before attending West
Point, had several experiences that illustrated how some CMTC
regulations often were loosely followed, if at all. He attended his
first camp at Plattsburg Barracks when he had barely turned 16—a
year underage. During the first week Armstrong "got into some
kind of trouble with my platoon leader," and as a result wasn't
recommended for the second year. By regulation, this should have
made him ineligible for the Red course in 1924. The next spring,

This candidate-drawn cartoon from the 1925 Camp Knox yearbook, The Mess Kit, *illustrates the youthful fad for calling each other "sheik."*

BRING A BUDDY, 1926!

Civilian Sheik—"What are you going to do next year?"
Military Sheik—"I'm coming to the 1926 CMTC and going to bring you along, Buddy."

however, he applied and was accepted to attend the July Plattsburg camp. Regulations also prohibited anyone from attending more than one camp a year. Young Armstrong, having learned that Artillery CMTC was being offered the next month at Madison Barracks, finished his Plattsburg training and took a bus to Madison Barracks—about 150 miles to the west—where he was accepted for the August camp.

By now Armstrong may have considered himself to be living proof that rules were made to be broken, causing him to ignore a rule of personal security that left him with a painful CMTC memory: "One day [at Madison Barracks] I went swimming in the lake and stuck my wallet with $30 in it under my pillow. It was gone when I returned to barracks."

The significance of the loss of $30 in the mid-1920s, particularly for a 17-year-old youth, can be appreciated by reading advertisements that appear in some CMTC yearbooks from those years. The Donald, a residential hotel outside Fort Snelling, advertised "A delightful, large, cool, spotlessly clean room, dressing room and bath apartment, *including breakfast and evening dinner* and complete modern hotel service" renting for $20 a week for one person, $30 for two, and $36 for three. An eight-ounce bottle of Coca-Cola® was a nickel; "Witching Hour Chocolates," available in one-, two- and five-pound boxes, sold for $1 a pound; a regulation, genuine-leather Sam Browne belt cost $5; and "Munson Last" army shoes were advertised at $4.50 to $6.50 a pair.[5]

On the other hand, the cost of a radio when compared to prices 70 years later seems inordinately expensive. The electronic miracle, almost unknown in 1920, by 1924–1925 had grown at an astonishing rate. The technology, however, was still in its infancy, and its manufacture and development were costly. A radio set made by Atwater Kent, one of the pioneer companies, could run between $200 and $300. Sets by Radiola were advertised for $35 to $425, and although the Radiola Super-Hetrodyne with a separate horn-shaped speaker was pictured with a handle, it was definitely not portable.[6] In fact, Army barracks and tents wouldn't resound to the racket of portable radios for at least another 20 years.

It appears that CMTC candidates in the mid-1920s had little or no exposure to radio during their month of training. A Camp Knox article on recreation stated: "Two large Service Clubs proved beacon lights for hundreds of candidates every night, equipped as they were with a piano, a phonograph with a large assortment of records, magazines and daily and weekly newspapers,"[7] but no mention of radio. There is the possibility, of course, that some lads brought the crystal sets they had assembled at home and after lights-out explored the dial in the privacy of their headsets.

As the decade neared its midway point, the roar of the "Roaring Twenties" picked up several hundred decibels. Compared to the explosion of radio, the automobile was the atomic blast of the decade. Paved roads were becoming common, as were filling stations and repair garages. Closed coaches and almost foolproof mechanisms reduced the hazards and discomfort of motoring.[8]

At the beginning of the decade not only had women won the right to vote but by 1925 Wyoming and Texas had each elected and inaugurated a woman as its governor. "Nice girls" now wore makeup, some even smoked cigarettes in public and drank cocktails, albeit illegally. The hemlines of skirts were rising as was the stock market and the market's popularity with average folks.

Fads were as numerous as weather changes and as short-lived, but moving pictures were here to stay. As the movies grew in popularity they increased in daring, until the industry, fearing government censorship, set up its own policing by installing former Postmaster General Will H. Hays to head what for many years would be called "the Hays Office."[9] But even with industry-imposed censorship, movies remained torrid enough not to cool down their popularity. Even though the movies were still silent, they sometimes lent new words to the language. Young American men, impressed with the impression Rudolph Valentino had made on American females with his movies, *The Sheik* and *Son of the Sheik*, adopted the nickname "sheik" (which was pronounced "sheek") for certain of their colleagues. CMTC candidates often awarded the title to selected barracks-mates—sometimes as praise, sometimes as sarcasm. A Camp Knox correspondent wrote: "There was a big turn out for the boat excursion [by] Co. G whose sheiks did their stuff as they do on the drill field and parade ground."[10]

Analyzing his fellow CMTCers at Fort Snelling a writer observed: "[Candidate] Dilling is the always present sheik—he parts his hair in the middle and lets it grow on the neck. Lang, according to his tales, is the local sheik 'back home.'"[11]

★

In 1925 the War Department took what it considered to be an innovative step: "The outstanding accomplishment of the 1925 Citizens' Military Training Camps was the success of the associate or 'parent' system of training. Under this system candidates are formed into additional subdivisions of existing tactical units of the Regular Army. This system operates to maintain the entity of Regular Army organizations. It gives opportunity for greater encouragement of competition among units and thereby builds up esprit and affords the candidates better instruction."[12]

Another development was reported by the Secretary of War: "During the summer of 1925 the policy of decentralization was continued for Citizens' Military Training Camps. Eleven additional posts were utilized to make a total of 40 camps." The report went on to say that mileage costs were reduced by increasing the number of camps, which "serves partially to offset the gradual yearly increase in per capita cost."[13]

Although in later paragraphs the report lists 41 camps, the inconsistency probably was because the earlier paragraph referred to 40 locations rather than scheduled CMTC camps. Two training camps were conducted at Plattsburg each summer. The number of participants continued to grow, with just over 57,000 young men applying and almost 34,000 attending the 1925 camps.[14]

With the conclusion of its fifth year, CMTC had come of age and could look forward to a bright future and continued growth. No one could have known, however, that its future was limited and its life one-quarter completed.

Horses and Mules

The average American youth of the 1920s and 1930s had limited association with four-legged transportation. By the early 1920s the horse was quickly disappearing from city streets and in small towns the horse population was dwindling. Farm boys were familiar with workhorses and mules, but horseback riding, at least in the Midwest and East, wasn't a way of life even for them. CMTC candidates, particularly those involved in cavalry and artillery training, therefore, were presented with another new experience and, sometimes, adventure.

Victor Vogel put into context the Army's devotion to horse flesh: "Long after the motor vehicle became commonplace in America the military services continued to use horses and mules, and World War II still found some army units depending on animals for transportation. Maybe it was because of economy, or simply reluctance to change, or maybe because of sentiment, but it took a long time to replace the stables with motor pools, and the horse soldier died hard."[1] For at least 18 of the 20 years of CMTC, horses and mules played a major and mostly unchanged role.

Candidates assigned to cavalry training at Camp Knox in 1922, however, had reason to wonder where the Army kept its horses. Camp Knox, not an active post at the time, had to bring in much of the training materiel for the 30 days of training. Apparently the requisition for the cavalry horses wasn't filled, causing some heavily satirical observations:

A TROOP?

Cadet Private Wheeler Q. Newton, Cavalry, Troop A
Members of Troop A, Cavalry are we
With drill the same as Infantry,
We walk and walk and never ride
For all we know the horses have died.
. . . .
But a happy bunch we happen to be
We boys of the Horseless Cavalry
All we have close to Horsemanship
Is a Colt to carry up on our hip.
. . . .
It's not so bad as it might be
The Cavalry of the C.M.T.C.
No horses to groom or saddles to clean
It's the laziest life I've ever seen.

No horses to watch or keep in line,
So give me the Cavalry every time
And if this camp is still standing here
You'll probably find us back next year.[2]

And a short essay titled "Horseless Are We" portrayed the plight of Troop C: "They say that the Legend of Sleepy Hollow has a 'Headless Horseman' in it. Well, Troop C was composed mainly of 'Horseless Horsemen' although some did act like they were headless too. We guys loved horses of course. Many of us had lived with them and had a sort of horse sense that is akin to relationship if you know what I mean. Of course, we wanted very much to ride the dumb brute—that's why we joined the Cavalry. It really wouldn't have been so bad if they would have furnished us with hobby horses and let us practice sitting in the saddles or putting our feet in the stirrups. Oh yes, the Colonel promised us plenty of stallions, mares, mules and colts of all kinds for next year but gosh! We may be all married by then and maybe our wives won't let us come.

"Shakespeare expressed our sentiments when he said, 'A horse, a horse! my kingdom for a horse!'

"You oughta hear Troop C singing the horseless blues!"[3] Many a young summertime soldier might have considered those Troop C troopers quite lucky. Take Tom Steele for instance: "I decided that riding horses was a far better way to travel than walking. However, there were many hot days at camp [Camp Mead, Maryland, 1936] when the horses were plenty hot and sweaty and we had to groom them including cleaning off the hooves before we could even get a drink of water. That was pure hell and didn't endear me toward the Artillery, and I even considered not coming back the next year."

"I was Infantry [Camp Ord, California, 1939, 1940]," said Joseph Watts. "My tent was backed by the Cav troop on the next company street. I'd be well on my way to dreamland before the Cav finished cleaning and feeding their horses after night exercises. The Artillery was horse-drawn so they had the same care and cleaning problem—my shoes hurt but that was minor compared to the horse-holders."

Like it or loathe it, the association with four-legged beasts was a learning experience. A paragraph in a camp yearbook described the early days of equestrian training: "After learning the fundamentals that precede riding we were allowed to saddle up and were taught how to mount. The mounting proved to be a regular slapstick comedy the first day but the improvement the second day was so marked that we hardly realized we were beginners. We had finally learned to mount and dismount and we were all anxiously awaiting the time when we would be allowed to ride our gallant nags. . . . The time finally did come and we were given a chance to try our luck on the back of our mount, some of us scared to death. The first ride was a thrill; even at a walk we were afraid of falling off the animal's back."[4]

Bruce Romick well remembered his lessons in the care and cleaning of horseflesh: "At the stables [Fort Des Moines, Iowa, 1939], we selected a horse that would be our mount and responsibility for the time in camp. We were taught to groom and clean the horse. The sergeant's instructions included 'Now take this cloth and wipe the horse's eyes, ears and dock.' Eyes and ears we understood—but 'What's the dock?' The sergeant demonstrated the technique of lifting the horse's tail and wiping the area below it. No great enthusiasm for this task was demonstrated by us trainees, but we did as told with no adverse effect on us or the horses. Some of the trainees hadn't ridden much and the McClellan saddles didn't seem to be padded in the right places. Some of us quickly learned the truth in the Infantry's nickname for the Cavalry—'blister butts.'"

Arnold Silver had similar memories of tending to his mount: "I remember that after riding the horses [Fort Oglethorpe, Georgia, 1933], we had to curry them, brush their coats, clean their hooves and clean out the docks. Then we had to shower to get the horses' hair off of us." Silver also had a pleasant memory of Sunday activity on horseback: "On Sunday mornings we were allowed to ride our horse on a supposed 'foxhunt' over the large reservation."

The McClellan saddle, mentioned by Bruce Romick, apparently was no more popular with cavalrymen than its namesake, the controversial Union general, George McClellan, was with President Lincoln. Here's what Hugh Graham had to say: "Having grown up on a farm I thought I knew how to ride a horse. Ha! All I knew was how to stay on. The McClellan saddle with the two-inch slit in the seat was a great incentive to become an officer and have a riding saddle [Fort Riley, Kansas, 1940]."

CMTC provided Gene Schueler with vivid memories of training as a mounted soldier: "We all rapidly discovered that the Army considered horses more valuable than men. Of course they had to be paid for while we were only 'rented.' We quickly found out that horses come before breakfast. Everything, food, water, cleaning. One day while being instructed [Fort McCoy, Wisconsin, 1935] on how to clean the horse's penis I asked, 'What did horses do before men were invented?' Not a diplomatic question to ask a grizzled old Regular Army sergeant. . . . While I had occasionally ridden horses before, this was a new experience. You held the

CMTC candidates in cavalry training weren't the only ones introduced to horsemanship. These candidates, taking field artillery training in 1923 at Fort Bliss, Texas, appear comfortable astride the horses hitched to a limber, a two-wheel cart that towed an artillery piece. (Photo by J. J. Gregor, Fort Bliss, Texas.)

reins in a certain way. You used only your left hand so as to keep the right hand available to draw the pistol on your hip. At least we didn't have swords. Our instructor was one of the best. A true Prussian type and I believe I still remember his name—Lt. Steiglitz. Lt. Steiglitz could sense if you even thought of raising your right hand from your side and his whip would come down on your wrist before you were aware of his presence."

Russ Haag transferred from Infantry to Cavalry his second year at the Presidio of Monterey and liked the change. "First day there we rode around the riding ring for two hours and developed a very sore butt," he said. "We enjoyed battalion parade at the end of the day when we would charge down the parade ground."

Many CMTC candidates were introduced to horses by being assigned to an Artillery unit. Darrel Rippeteau explained the function of horses in the Artillery: "[The French 75-mm howit-zers] were pulled by six horses, three teams, and my first assign-ment was the 'wheel team' and I rode on the right horse [Fort Snelling, 1935]."

"I was the brakeman [Ft. Hoyle, Maryland, 1938] on the limber [a two-wheel cart that towed the gun] from which I got a good workout," remembered Clyde Boden. "My horse was Elhazard. I learned initially that the horse had to be completely taken care of before I did anything."

"Because of my high school cadet corps background I went in as a 'second-year' man [Fort Hoyle, 1928] and it was assumed that I had previous field artillery experience," recalled Robert William-son. "Truth was I hardly knew one end of a horse from the other, but I was assigned a 'wheel team.' I soon learned to put the bit in the mouth and the crouper under the tail. Riding and guiding the team was something else. My first time out I got my legs between the horse and the traces and could hardly walk when I dismounted, to say nothing of a problem sitting."

Experience with horses certainly made its mark on one CMTC candidate: "My love of the horse was nurtured [the Presidio of Monterey, 1932–1935] and has become a lifelong project as can be shown by years of equine veterinary practice topped by being the chief veterinary officer at the XXIII Olympiad in Los Angeles," said Dr. William Ommert.

As a candidate at Fort Ethan Allen, Vermont, in the latter years of CMTC, Dirk van der Voet had a choice between Cavalry and Field Artillery, which by this time was towed by mechanical rather than animal means. For van der Voet it was an easy decision: "Horses and I reached an agreement in my younger years as a visitor on a Vermont farm—we'd go our separate ways and have nothing to do with each other."

Mules weren't as numerous as horses, but their strong personal traits made them every bit as unforgettable as their cousins in the Cavalry and Artillery. Arthur Hyman from Xenia, Ohio, and a member of Co. M, 10th Infantry (the machine gun company just as all companies M were in those days), wrote of the mules he met at Camp Knox:

"We got a lot of fun and work by associating with our friends, the mules. We city slickers encountered something new when it came to harnessing and cleaning them, but within a few days we were not to be outdone by the more experienced country lads. The sad part about our friends, the mules, was that they just didn't seem to go when we wanted them to. We shall never forget the day one became tired of army life, and decided to go A.W.O.L. Quite a chase ensued before the brute was caught and safe in his harness."[5]

Bill Bentson, who was assigned to machine guns at Vancouver Barracks, Washington, recalled a similar experience: "The machine guns were mounted on a two-wheel cart pulled by cantankerous mules. Most cadets in the machine gun company had never handled mules in their lifetime and the mules sensed this. . . . One afternoon the machine gun company was filing down a slight hill, when all of a sudden, one of the mules was spooked and took off down the hill and having broken loose from the handler was given a free run. The cart was flying through the air and bouncing around with ammunition boxes and machine gun parts flying in all directions. The gun and cart were a total write-off by the time they subdued the frenzied beast."

The young troopers at Camp Dix, perhaps with the Military Academy at West Point in mind, adopted a Dix mule as their mascot. "Bunk" may have been as contrary as any of his brethren, but at least he was silent about it. Smuggled back to this country after World War I, Bunk was brayless, having been deprived of his vocal mechanism by military veterinarians—just as were other Army mules shipped to France to prevent any "hee-haws" from revealing the unit's position.[6]

Archie Stewart said the mules at Fort Sill, Oklahoma, at times were sharper than their candidate drivers: "I remember the mules that pulled the machine gun carts [1936] knew which way to turn when the sergeant called 'SQUAD RIGHT, CART RIGHT,' but we didn't know. The mules required a lot of manicuring after the drills."

Here's what novelist Ernest K. Gann recalled of his experience with mules while attending Fort Snelling's CMTC in the late 1920s: "Only infinite patience made a true mule-skinner of a mere man and it took a rare personality to long tolerate the look of superiority on their bland faces. Mules serving their hitch in the United States Army did not give a damn about the course of battle, simulated or otherwise. Their attitude greatly enriched a trooper's vocabulary."[7]

Marco Thorne experienced firsthand the special regard the Army had for its four-legged companions: "Once at Monterey we had to stand parade at retreat for two horses that were being retired. Mules and horses were considered as privates and like humans deserved a parade in their honor when retirement came. They were put to pasture for the remainder of their lives and had good care."

Still Around and Getting Bigger

1 9 2 6 – 1 9 3 0

Six years old and thriving, CMTC was awarded its own organizational flag by the War Department in 1926—demonstrating the department's recognition of CMTC as an official member of the Army family. A *New York Times* story reported the event in the high-school-journalism style the distinguished journal sometimes fell victim to: "Time-honored and battle-worn flags in the U.S. Army's official gallery opened ranks to admit a 'recruit' yesterday. This youngest addition to the long line of army colors and standards is a regimental flag which Secretary of War [Dwight F.] Davis has just authorized for units of the Citizens' Military Training Camps.

"It is a blue flag with an eagle in white rising with outspread wings and the letters C.M.T.C. also in white. A knotted fringe of yellow silk borders the flag while attached to the spearhead of the staff is a tasseled cord of red, white and blue strands.

"The C.M.T.C. flag will be carried at 50 C.M.T.C. encampments throughout the country where 35,000 volunteer youths will be in training this Summer."[1]

The writer's numbers were almost right. The War Department reported 49 camps in operation in 1926 with 34,194 attending. Nine new posts were added as part of the Army's continuing program of decentralizing the training to reduce mileage costs. "Decentralizing served partially to offset the gradual increase in per capita cost, because of depletion of war stocks," the War Department reported.[2]

The ever-loyal-to-the-cause *Times*—75 years old in 1926—declared in a July headline, "Army Will Train More Boys at Less Cost." The story said CMTC appropriations "are $2,505,128, a reduction of $212,000 over last year." According to the *Times* the number of young men to be trained in 1926 "is an increase of about 2,100 over last year." Attendance was up but according to the War Department's figures about 7,000 fewer applications were submitted for 1926 than 1925.[3]

The *New York Times* and CMTC weren't alone in observing significant birthdays; the United States was 150 years old in 1926. To celebrate the event Philadelphia held the Sesquicentennial Exposition from June through November.

In that sixth summer of Citizens' Military Training Camps three sons of prominent men made the newspapers in connection with the program. John Coolidge, who had attended CMTC at Camp Devens for two years, announced he wouldn't be returning for a third year. The President's son, a sophomore at Amherst College, instead had signed up for summer school at the University of Vermont to study economics.[4] But the program also would gain two sons of famous men. The Secretary of War's son, Dwight F. Davis, Jr., would attend Devens that summer, where he would enter as a "private like all other youths," his father said, adding that "no favors of any kind were [to] be extended to him."[5]

Warren E. Pershing, son of General Pershing, became a first-year candidate at Fort Snelling.[6] Donald Smythe wrote: "Pershing was concerned that Warren [who, according to Smythe, was 16 at the time] not grow up a snobbish kid, the spoiled son of a famous father. He urged attendance at a summer training camp, both to see what military life was like and, more importantly, to mix with a different class of person than he was encountering at a private boys' school."[7]

It also was a year for top government leaders to pay calls on

CMTC sessions. New York Governor Al Smith, who in March had issued a public statement endorsing the program, visited the July Plattsburg camp. This camp, the first of two camps held at Plattsburg that summer, was restricted to first-year men. During his visit Governor Smith watched Basic candidates from companies A and L play a baseball game umpired by Army Reserve Lt. Col. Theodore Roosevelt, Jr.[8]

The August Plattsburg camp, attended by candidates of all four years, was inspected by the President himself. The always succinct Coolidge, having scrutinized a CMTC mess hall menu, said, "They can't famish on that."[9]

Also in August, the Associated Press reported Vice President Charles G. Dawes saying, "That's the right idea. Let us have more of it," as he watched 2,000 CMTC men pass in review at Fort Sheridan, Illinois. During the ceremony the Vice President presented 50 medals to candidates for special achievement.[10]

★

The peak year for CMTC was 1927, with 53 camps conducted in the 9 corps areas, including Puerto Rico. The War Department's annual report, which at last began to clearly identify enrollment and completion figures, listed 39,798 reporting and 38,597 completing.[11] Although for the next several years the War Department's annual quotas were slightly in excess of 40,000, "no-shows" and failures during in-processing physicals prevented 1927's high numbers from ever being reached again.

President Harding's dream of 100,000 youths being trained each year remained just a dream. The War Department, however, seemed convinced that had adequate funds ever been appropriated, the number of applicants would have soared. The Secretary of War wrote: "Even this considerable number of applications [58,007 for 1928][12] does not afford an accurate indication of the widespread popularity of this system of military, physical, and moral training. In many corps areas and States the allotted quotas were oversubscribed from two to three months prior to the opening of the camps, such oversubscription necessitating immediate notice that further applications could not receive favorable consideration."[13]

Young men heading for CMTC the summer of 1927 might have carried their chests just a bit higher from the vicarious pride they felt over the accomplishments of an American of their own generation. Charles A. Lindbergh, a 25-year-old from Minnesota, on May 21 had shocked the world and made Americans delirious with his solo flight across the Atlantic. Frederick Lewis Allen illustrated the mood of the country on May 20 as Lindbergh began his journey: "Young and old, rich and poor, farmer and stockbroker, Fundamentalist and skeptic, highbrow and lowbrow, all with one accord fastened their hopes upon the young man in the *Spirit of St. Louis.* To give a single instance of the intensity of their mood: at the Yankee Stadium in New York, where the Maloney-Starkey fight was held on the evening of the 20th, forty thousand hard-boiled boxing fans rose as one man and stood with bared heads in impressive silence when the announcer asked them to pray for Lindbergh."[14]

Here was a young man who, earlier in the decade, might have been a CMTC candidate, had he chosen, suddenly earning the world's adoration. Lindbergh's name must have been mentioned countless times in CMTC barracks and mess halls that summer. Two CMTC alumni each recalled taking part during their camps in an event involving Lindbergh. Ernest Gann told of taking a chance on volunteering for a 30-man detail his sergeant called for: "By volunteering . . . I became one of the troopers assigned to protect Charles Lindbergh when he landed at Minneapolis after his flight to Paris."[15]

David Gray had this memory of "Lucky Lindy" (a news-media nickname Lindbergh hated[16]): "One morning on short notice we were all assembled on a broad, wide-open area then known as Roosevelt Ridge [at Camp Knox] which later became the post airfield [Godman Field]. That spring Lindbergh had made his

Col. Theodore Roosevelt, Jr. posed for a candidate's Kodak® at the 1928 Plattsburg CMTC. During the program's 20 years Col. Roosevelt spent several of his two-week Organized Reserve Corps training periods as a CMTC commander. (Photo courtesy of Sol Fenichel.)

memorable flight and afterwards toured the U.S. as part of the nation's celebration of his flight. We were told that he would be leaving Louisville shortly and would fly over our location on his way west. Sure enough he not only flew over, but circled and buzzed us for a few minutes before flying on, waving out the window. His plane was never meant for stunting, but he made it seem as if it were. I knew nothing about aircraft but I could tell by the way he handled it that he was sure one helluva pilot and his Atlantic flight was 98 percent his skill, 2 percent luck. It was the single most exciting event that happened to us."

Although nothing could top Lindbergh's feat, sports and enter-tainment continued to fascinate the nation. Nothing was of any greater interest to American lads than sports and "moving picture shows." After losing his heavyweight title the year before to Gene Tunney, Jack Dempsey, in a July 1927 Yankee Stadium fight, floored Jack Sharkey on his way to attempt reclaiming the title. In the September rematch with ex-Marine Tunney at Chicago's Soldier Field, Dempsey failed to regain the crown in the legendary and controversial bout of the "long count." Eight days later sports fans went wild when on September 30, Yankee outfielder, George Herman ("Babe") Ruth hit his 60th home run of the year in a game against the Boston Red Sox.

That year, 1927, also was a signal year for the U.S. motion picture industry. *The Jazz Singer*, starring Al Jolson, became the best-known among the "talkies" pioneer films, technically crude as it was. This was the year the Academy of Motion Picture Arts and Sciences was founded and began its annual award of the Oscars. Top awards went to *Seventh Heaven*, starring Janet Gaynor, and *Wings*, one of the best of many movies about the late war, which had become a popular movie subject. The young men attending CMTC, however, were more apt to have seen some of the popular films of the year before—silent films such as *Beau Geste*, with Ronald Colman and Noah Beery, *Ben Hur*, or *Black Pirate*, starring Douglas Fairbanks, Sr.

In July of 1927 the man who began it all, Maj. Gen. Leonard Wood, now Governor-General of the Philippines, observed the opening day of the Plattsburg camp. A month later he died in a Boston hospital. Memorial services were held throughout those CMTC camps still in session as the program's virtual founder and strongest individual supporter was buried in Arlington Cemetery.[17]

The week before Wood's death, President Coolidge, once more a man of few words, said: "I do not choose to run for President in 1928."—end of subject.[18]

★

The average CMTC candidate of 1928 probably didn't feel much involvement in the presidential race that year, other than the traditional after-lights-out barracks arguments. Herbert Hoover won the Republican nomination in June at the Kansas City convention. Those Americans who wanted to see the "Coolidge Prosperity" continue strongly supported Hoover. Al Smith, governor of New York and a Roman Catholic, received the Democrats' nod at the convention in Dallas, also in June. Many in the traditionally Democratic "Solid South," for the first time, split their ticket and voted Republican, fearing that a Catholic chief-executive would take orders from the Vatican.

The 1928 CMTC program changed little from the year before. Attendance fell to 35,658, with 34,514 completing, although 41,007 men had been issued orders and applications had hit a record 58,007. Fifty-two camps were held, one fewer than the year before. The Engineer Corps course at Fort Du Pont, Delaware, was discontinued in 1927 because, as the *New York Times* put it, "It has been found that it is hardly practicable to train engineer officers in the Citizens' Military Training Camps, on account of the large amount of technical instruction involved."[19]

The War Department announced its intention to increase the number of reserve officers at the camps.[20] From its inception in 1921 selected reserve officers had participated as CMTC cadre. In 1928 the number was greatly increased, with entire Organized Army Reserve regiments—skeleton units made up mostly of officers—serving during two of the four weeks of training. Theodore Roosevelt, Jr., by then a full colonel, returned to Plattsburg for a second year of duty. Later, as a brigadier general, Roosevelt participated in the Allied landings in France in World War II and died of an illness a few days later. He had been a charter member of the Plattsburg movement in 1915.[21]

★

In 1929 the War Department made another adjustment to the program by dropping Basic CMTC courses in Cavalry, Field Artillery, and Signal Corps, decreeing that all first-year men would receive basic Infantry training.[22]

Herbert Clark Hoover became the 31st President of the United States, having predicted the end of poverty in the nation with "a chicken in every pot, a car in every garage." Although easy to dismiss as political hyperbole, few in early 1929 could have guessed the bitter irony the slogan would hold before Hoover's administration was half completed.

Among the nearly 38,000 young Americans who were headed for a month of CMTC training at 53 camps in 1929, the stock market probably wasn't of much concern. There were more important things to occupy young people's minds that year. Tin Pan Alley was turning out lots of (in the parlance of the day) *swell* popular songs; and movies were getting better than ever. Many camp shower rooms must have echoed with raucous renditions of "I Can't Give You Anything But Love," or "There's a Rainbow Round My Shoulder," or maybe even some imitations (properly nasal) of Rudy Vallee's current hit, "I'm Just a Vagabond Lover." Since the Army Motion Picture Service didn't begin installing sound equipment in its theaters until early 1930, if a candidate in 1929 wanted to see one of Hollywood's new musicals, *Gold Diggers of Broadway* or *Rio Rita,* it would have to be on weekends off post.*

The big stock market crash didn't occur until October 24—"Black

---

*In 1929 the Motion Picture Service declined to install sound in its theaters because "the sound equipment on the market at present does no appear to have reached that state of perfection" which was expected in the near future. In 1930 sound was installed in 47 theaters and by 1931 "talkies" were playing in 74 Army movie houses. Sources: *War Department Annual Reports* for 1929 (p. 253), 1930 (p. 367), and 1931 (p. 225).

Thursday"—and few could imagine it was just the first shock of an economic earthquake that would shake the entire world and deal out misery for the next ten years.

The stock market crash didn't adversely affect 1930 CMTC attendance. Again 53 camps were run, with almost 38,000 men completing the course.[23] Recruiting was becoming easier all the time. It would take two years for the shock waves of the crash to reach CMTC, and then the life would be nearly shaken out of the program.

Fun and Games

If Napoleon Bonaparte's vanquisher, the Duke of Wellington, actually said, "The battle of Waterloo was won on the playing fields of Eton," he expressed a philosophy warmly embraced by the U.S. Army between the World Wars. During the 1920s and 1930s competitive team sports were an important part of the day-to-day training regimen of Regular Army soldiers. The Army made athletic activities an even more predominant part of the daily life of its youthful summertime charges, the CMTC candidates.

When on garrison duty a regular soldier spent only half the day on military subjects. "Weekday afternoons were devoted to cleaning up grounds or equipment or other housekeeping chores," wrote Victor Vogel in *Soldiers of the Old Army*. "Team sports were popular, and there was usually an athletic contest in the afternoons. If a man did not have any other duty he could be found on the athletic field."[1] Even if it had been normal for the Regular Army to pursue military subjects for 8 to 10 hours a day, such a schedule wouldn't have been considered appropriate for the youths attending CMTC, who were the Army's virtual guests for four weeks. Other than kitchen police (K.P.), which was considered an important part of military indoctrination, CMTC candidates weren't called on to perform many company or garrison fatigue details. The Army went to considerable efforts to schedule a variety of athletic activities each duty day, as well as off-duty recreational events, both on and off post.

The 1925 CMTC baseball championship team at Camp Knox posed for the yearbook with its mascot, a bull terrier. The dog (or its twin brother) also posed with the runner-up team. Baseball had no rival as a team sport with CMTC. For several years Babe Ruth contributed an autographed baseball and bat to be awarded to the top player at each CMTC program throughout the nation. (Photo from the 1925 Camp Knox CMTC yearbook, The Mess Kit.)

The Fort Monroe CMTC newspaper, *The Salvo,* outlined the policy on athletics, which seems to have been the standard for CMTC through its existence: "Supervised athletics are scheduled for approximately three hours every day. The athletic program begins each morning with calisthenics, in which exactness and precision of healthful exercise will be emphasized. In the afternoons each candidate, depending on his abilities and desires, will be required to participate in swimming, baseball, tennis, volleyball, boxing or some supervised athletic activity. . . . During camp each of the four teams from the four batteries will organize in different sports to compete for camp awards."[2]

No single subject took up more space in camp yearbooks than did the photographs and written accounts of sporting events. Many of the medals and awards handed out at graduation ceremonies were in recognition of athletic accomplishments. Wilfred Menegus said he won a bronze medal at Plattsburg Barracks in 1924 "which I value to this day" for finishing eighth out of 300 runners in a five-mile cross-country race. John Moale, who took CMTC at the Presidio of San Francisco in 1937, remembered a final track meet held at Kezar Stadium, San Francisco's major outdoor sports field at the time: "I received a medal for being a member of a winning relay team."

Dr. Richard Matteson, a veterinarian from Indiana, disdained the plethora of medals presented for sports at the expense of more important military skills. "At the ending awards parade [Camp Custer, Michigan, 1940] men were called forth by name and given baseball awards and trophies," Matteson recalled. "Not a man was recognized in any way for marksmanship. Since France had fallen two months before, I thought their emphasis was wrong. This was military training, not 'jock' ball games." Matteson was "second highest machine gunner and had raw fingers from practice." He said he practiced gun drill with a regular soldier on Saturday afternoons and Sundays.

For Russell Price, at Fort Meade in 1939, the chance to compete in an individual sport taught him an object lesson he never forgot: "The one thing I could do well was swim, so they entered me in this one-mile meet. . . . I found myself leading the race—no one was even near me—so in sight of the finish line, I let up a bit and the man behind just flew by me. I came in second but that was the last time I ever slackened off in anything I do."

Among athletic events involving one-on-one competition boxing always vied for top position in popularity. Not all candidates could, or wished to qualify for bouts; but anyone could be a spectator. At Camp Knox in the early 1920s the matches were held at night under the lights, drawing the maximum number of spectators and also taking care that if a boxer fell it was from a fist and not the boiling afternoon sun.

Although no rival of boxing in spectator interest, tennis was a favorite at some camps. "Tennis was probably the most popular sport in the CMT Camp this summer. There were ten courts, and during off-hours all of them were usually filled. Even those who did not qualify for the singles or doubles enjoyed playing, and seventy-four men qualified for the singles and almost twice that many for the doubles events."[3]

Athletic games weren't the sole component of the fun and games offered at the various camps. CMTC yearbooks, newspapers, and the reminiscences of alumni tell of scheduled off-duty activities, which, for 20 years, were similar from coast to coast. Among them were weekend dances, trips to the beach or off-post events, band concerts, and troop talent shows.

The frequency of post dances doesn't seem to have been standard, however. Maxwell Hamilton wrote: "At night, there were dances most evenings [Plattsburg Barracks, 1927] with partners made up of waitresses and students from a summer school then in session down the road a piece, movies, boxing matches and even band concerts under the stars."[4] But at Madison Barracks, New York, the candidates at the 1933 camp were limited to just one scheduled dance: "The long-awaited CMTC dance was held Saturday evening, August 27th at the Post Gymnasium. Music was furnished by the 5th F.A. Band. The boys were all slicked up to greet the girls who came in from Watertown and Sackets [*sic*] Harbor. The girls were very friendly, and the only complaint was that the dance was held too late in the month to permit the boys to date the new acquaintances they made."[5]

Camp officials seemed to have no difficulty in finding local young women who were willing to attend post dances for the summertime soldiers. The Army's civilian women employed as camp service club hostesses undoubtedly played a large part in arranging groups of females and convincing parents to allow their daughters to attend. Transportation and chaperons were required, of course. Dave Taylor remembered: "As Blue students, we would beg the Reserve Army officers for their Sam Browne belts to wear at Friday night dances, when the Army would bring girls from Spokane, in Army Dodge 1933 model half-ton trucks with canvas covers."

Bill Bentson remembered a dance at Vancouver Barracks in the late 1930s where the chaperons suddenly found themselves with no one to chaperon: "There was a four-alarm fire about a mile from camp and the sky was lit up for miles. Most of us grabbed a gal and ran to the fire and this broke up the dance. We didn't return to the camp too early that night."

James Duncan's memory of women visiting Jefferson Barracks, Missouri, in 1940 is intriguing in its possible implications: "At early evening on the parade grounds we would socialize with the young ladies who came from St. Louis. All very innocent from my perspective at the time—but in later years I realized it was not always so. But I was a 16-year-old country boy who really did not know much about the world. It was really an age of innocence for me."

Bud Rubel, an alumnus of Fort McClellan, Alabama, confirmed that candidates in the South also were treated to weekend dances. "Saturday night dances were held in the service club with a few bus loads of girls from Anniston there at the dance."

Sometimes those who played such an important role in arranging the dances—the service club hostesses—were themselves a special attraction for the candidates. "I remember an untouchable young lady named Trixie Lawler, who each year worked at the recreational building, had thousands of us madly in love with her," said James Cantwell of his three years at Fort Sheridan, Illinois, in the late 1930s.

Candidates at one Fort Niagara, New York, camp were treated to a special social occasion, as described in this *New York Times* account: "The home and lawn of Colonel and Mrs. G. E. Stewart at Fort Niagara was aglow tonight in entertainment of the students of the Cit Mil Tng Cp. [*sic*]. In a comfortable spot, the fine band of the Twenty-eighth Inf. was quartered, adding materially to the scene and activity.

"From neighboring cities and villages a number of young women had been invited to aid in making the social feature of the 1929 camp memorable in the minds of those in attendance."[6]

Movies were available every night; usually for a few nickels at the post theater, or sometimes open-air theaters where little or nothing was charged. David Gray said that at Camp Knox in 1927 some of his barracks mates from the mountains of eastern Kentucky and West Virginia had never seen a movie. "I recall one lad in particular with the incongruous first name of Cicero who never missed a showing the entire encampment."

Newspapers published for and by CMTC candidates regularly ran the week's schedule of movies, which was not only a service to readers but made convenient filler material. From the Fort Sill newspaper: "TONIGHT: Anton Walbrock and Margot Grahame in 'The Soldier and the Lady,' admission 20 cents. Trucks leave Hostess House at 6:15 P.M."[7]

Activities were also available for those who had rather entertain than be entertained. In the same issue from Fort Sill under "Co. A Reports" the question was asked, "Don't you think the boy who danced and that French-harp [harmonica] player on last night's 1st Battalion Stunt Nite program were good?"

Al Gold, "Cub Reporter, 1st Class" of *The Little Bearcat*, the Presidio of Monterey CMTC paper, wrote: "Our Hostess wants to make a strong appeal for anyone and everyone who has had or is interested in dramatics or anything in that line. Many boys have already signed up and there is room for many and many more. So be sure and see the Hostess some time as soon as possible and be sure to sign up. Miss Trickler has available for use a complete costume wardrobe with everything that goes to make an entertainment go over. The Hostess Room is open from 11:30 A.M. to Tattoo at night so there is plenty of time to speak to her.

"???SINGERS::: Stop torturing your company and sign up for

the boy's Troubadour Club. Miss Trickler, the camp hostess, has gone to much trouble to obtain good music books and prepare for this club. I will help you singers who need practice and experience.

"'Stunt Nights' scheduled for every night between July 20 and 29. . . ."[8]

A newspaper from the 1939 Fort Monroe CMTC provided candidates who wanted to sing with the words to songs such as "Dinah," "K-K-K-Katy," "Let Me Call You Sweetheart," "That Old Gang of Mine," "The Sidewalks of New York," and "The Man on the Flying Trapeze."[9]

An event possibly equal in popularity to the on-post dance with imported female partners was the planned off-post trip. Who doesn't enjoy leaving the confines of classroom, camp, or office for a special sojourn? Trips of this kind made a lasting impression on many who contributed memories to this book:

• "Each camp made one trip to Salinas for the rodeo [one of the nation's prominent rodeos, which is still in existence], using World War I four-wheel drive, hard-tired trucks at about 10 MPH." —*Willis Bliss.*

• "There is a beach north of Monterey near what is now Seaside. We swam there and sunbathed there on the squeaky white sand. It was all in the nude. No women showed up when we were there on Saturday or Sunday; they knew better. We called the place Bareass Beach." —*Marco Thorne.*

• "It was the normal practice through my Blue year for the Army to charter one of the vessels operating between the Long Beach-San Pedro docks and Catalina Island for an all-day outing for the candidates and cadre." —*Frank Gregory.*

• "We were taken to big league baseball games [St. Louis Cardinals and Browns] on an excursion steamer on the Mississippi." —*Estes Proffer.*

• "There were Wednesday trips to West Point and the Yankee stadium and meeting with the great Babe Ruth." —*Stan Milkowski.*

• "A special Baltimore & Ohio train took us [1,500 candidates] to Washington, D.C., for a baseball game where we detrained and were marched to Griffith Stadium about one and a half miles away. Our band serenaded us and other spectators." —*Jack Reeside.*

• "In 1939 we went to a baseball game at the [New York] Polo Grounds, marching from the dock to the Polo Grounds behind a band and with a police escort. Talk about big shots! By this time I was a squad leader." —*Chester Carpenter.*

Being a member of an all-candidate CMTC band sometimes could provide the young musicians with special opportunities. In 1925 Camp Knox CMTC band members (the first band made up of CMTC candidates was reputed to have been organized at Camp Knox in 1923[10]) were guests of the old Louisville *Herald-Post* newspaper, where they played a late afternoon concert in a Louisville park, were given dinner at the YMCA cafeteria, and, before playing another evening concert at the same, park were astonished to find their picture on the front page of the *Herald-Post*'s late edition.[11]

In the late 1920s and early 1930s recruiters from the Sixth Corps Area began signing up as many members as possible of bands from high schools in Michigan. A band of about 40 pieces from Bay City provided the marching music at Fort Brady, Michigan, in 1929, and a 144-man band from a Grand Rapids high school was the official CMTC band at Fort Sheridan, Illinois, the next year.[12]

The music at post dances and evening concerts was most often provided by Regular Army bands, which were as professional as any listener could ask for. By the mid-1930s "swing" bands were becoming the rage, and Army band leaders weren't timid about "borrowing" arrangements from some of the leading jazz orchestras such as the Benny Goodman, Tommy Dorsey, "Chick" Webb, and Erskine Hawkins groups and laying down credible renditions of the hits of the day. Bruce Armstrong remembered the dance band from the First Division playing Dorsey's arrangements of

"Marie" and "Song of India" before the start of the evening outdoor movie. Dave Taylor said the Fourth Infantry's dance band at Vancouver Barracks introduced him to the thrill of live big-band music by playing "Johnson Rag," "Wah-Wah Blues," and other popular tunes.

★

No doubt the military training and discipline provided by the Army wasn't enjoyed by all, or even a majority, of the young CMTC candidates. It's fortunate that those who planned and ran Citizens' Military Training Camps were successful in coming up with recreational activities that would please all the candidates and placate those who didn't quite relish military ways.

17

On the Town

No matter how good a job the Army did in planning off-duty activities for CMTC candidates, on weekends many lads were still eager to look for off-post adventures. Camp officials didn't have much reason, however, to worry about allowing most candidates out on their own: the combination of youthful inexperience, lack of funds, and limited mobility acted as a "governor," dampening the speed these young human engines might generate. Not that many didn't try to sample the sensuality and sin reputed to be out there for the taking just beyond the post gate. Marco Thorne remembered some of these attractions in Monterey, California, during the early 1930s: "Monterey had a depression because the sardines no longer ran in nearby ocean waters and Cannery Row [written about by John Steinbeck] was beginning to fade. In his book, *Sweet Thursday,* in one of the stories Steinbeck speaks of a well-known town madam whom he calls Dora. Her real name was Flora and she had a place called Flora's Woods. The Army told her that if she admitted any CMTC candidates (we wore the high collar World War I blouses) they would close her down. She'd sit on the front porch of her place, men's private parts tattooed on her open chest and tell us to go away, 'Please.'"

Thorne said even though Prohibition was still in effect, "We could get a pint of homemade Chianti in a little house on Pacific Grove Avenue for 25 cents. If one didn't get drunk, one got sick on the stuff. It had a real kick."

Eugene Salet told of one of his company officers at Fort Douglas, Utah, a Lt. Sheetz, leading Salet and two of his buddies on a weekend bacchanal they would probably never have managed by themselves. Salet had been impressed with the officer, and he and his two friends were flattered when the lieutenant invited the three candidates to accompany him to Salt Lake City for the weekend. This turned out to be a mistake that Salet never forgot, and an event long rued, probably, by Lt. Sheetz, a reserve officer on active duty. Perhaps it was a civilian outlook the lieutenant hadn't yet shed that made him consider these three inexperienced youths as his contemporaries.[1]

Off to Salt Lake City on the Saturday afternoon of the camp's third week the group rented two adjoining rooms in one of the city's best hotels. The first stop was dinner at a good restaurant and then a visit to a nightclub. Even though this was Salt Lake City in the late 1920s, Prohibition and the heavy Mormon influence didn't keep the club owner from selling liquor, or populating the place with friendly females who were there to stimulate the sale of drinks. Salet and his friends ordered peach brandy, a familiar first choice—often later regretted—of young novice drinkers. "As we sat sipping our brandy, several of the bar girls made their initial approaches," Salet recalled. After buying drinks for the women and each ordering a second brandy, the young men invited their new friends to dance. With the first dance finished the women asked for another drink. It wasn't until much later, Salet said, that the three candidates realized the "ladies" were being served colored water while they were drinking the real stuff. In the meantime Lt. Sheetz had latched on to the female of his choice and "paid very little attention to us" for the rest of the stay at the nightclub.

After about four brandies each and with their leader preoccupied with his new love, the besotted boys managed to make it to the hotel rooms and the bathroom where the peach brandy took its final effect. The next morning after drugged but sound sleep the only thing left of the brandies were collective headaches. The peach brandy highs were gone, but so was Lt. Sheetz. The three spent the day sightseeing in Salt Lake and returned to the hotel lobby at 5 P.M. expecting to connect with the lieutenant since they were supposed to be back at camp in another hour. Sheetz didn't appear until eight o'clock when, as he greeted the three panicking candidates, he "mustered all the dignity he could and said he appreciated that we had waited for him." By using his rank to intimidate the guard at the Fort Douglas gate, Lt. Sheetz provided a diversion that allowed the three lads to sneak in and make it to their barracks before bed check. Salet said the experience was his first lesson in the leadership principle that there is "no way that officers and enlisted men could fraternize and maintain respect for each other."

Without further elaboration Russell Eberhardt, who attended CMTC in the Midwest in the early 1930s, said: "We all had our experiences with bootleggers and camp followers." Probably so, but among the contributors to this book only Pat Herst provided a story approaching Salet's for flirting with sins of the flesh: "We always talked of visiting Vancouver's red-light district [in the late 1920s]. One time five or six of us drew straws to see who would visit the whore and we all went to the place and rang the bell. The woman came to the door happy to see so many potential customers. We explained that only one of us was to be accommodated, with the others watching. She said it could not be done, that only one could go to bed with her and that she would take care of the others one by one. We balked at this, for most of us were too frightened to go ahead and she told us to go away and to come back in two years."

Undoubtedly others visited neighborhoods where the prospects for sin looked promising. Gerold Breuer, an alumnus of Fort Benjamin Harrison's training in 1928 and 1929, recalled visits to Ohio St. in Indianapolis, an avenue offering establishments not on any mothers' approved lists.

William Huntley and his friends committed a slight and harmless violation of regulations on weekends while attending Fort Snelling. "When we were on pass [1935] we were expected to wear our wool shirts, cotton britches, wool wrap leggings and a wool overseas cap. They weren't very dressy. We had left some civilian clothes at my cousin's, so we would stop there, change clothes, and feel more human than we would have in those hot uniforms."

Edward Randall and his buddies in the late 1920s had a plan to circumvent Prohibition, the regulation on civilian clothes, and restriction to camp on weeknights: "Fort Brady in Sault Sainte Marie was across from Sault Sainte Marie, Canada. Canada was 'wet,' Michigan was 'dry.' We kept civilian clothes at a nearby hotel for a few cents charge. After retreat, we'd change to civvies and head for Canada. The ferry was six cents and beer was a nickel (or maybe the reverse). We'd catch the last ferry back, and run up the hill two miles to make bed check. Fun!"

In the early days of Plattsburg Barracks' CMTC, according to Donald Armstrong's memory, candidates were sometimes allowed off post on weeknights, but once in town they were still hardly at liberty. "We CMTCers would ride the trolley downtown in the evening and wander around trying to look like soldiers. This was only five years after the end of World War I and the streets were patrolled by pairs of acting MPs from the 26th Infantry, many of them hard-bitten veterans of the toughest fighting in France," he said. "Those patrolling in Plattsburg kept us in line by strictly enforcing such rules as no hands in pockets and we couldn't even look cross eyed at the girls."

The Madison Barracks CMTC newspaper told the story of three candidates stumbling upon a group of friendly females in nearby Carthage, New York. The three stopped in at a Knights of Columbus hall where a roomful of young women were attending a presentation on Westinghouse appliances given by what the writer described as "an entrancing young lady (brunette—and we have her dated 'til the end of camp)." The candidates were shown to "seats of honour [*sic*]" by one of the women, and then observed "with great interest, the process of constructing an intriguing strawberry meringue cake."[2]

It was neither illicit liquor nor the lure of ladies that tempted Pat Herst and his tent-mate to risk big trouble by sneaking out to Vancouver after bed check. It was sports, of a sort, and money. "My tent-mate one year was a professional wrestler. Vancouver had professional wrestling and one popular wrestler was called Tiger McCann. My tent-mate was on the card as 'brother of Tiger McCann.' He wasn't related to the real McCann. One of the nights he was slated to wrestle we waited for bedcheck which was about 9 P.M. We dressed and sneaked off post through a broken wire fence. He got $10 every time he wrestled."

Most of the off-post experiences recounted here aren't what General Pershing had in mind back in 1921 when he told the assembled CMTC candidates at Fort Snelling: "I hope all of you young men can return at the end of this camp and tell your fathers and mothers that you had a clean good time, that all of you, you and your mates, lived clean and moral lives." Chances are few, if any, of the mothers and fathers of our contributors were told the stories recounted here—at least not until after a few years. But it seems likely that Black Jack Pershing wouldn't have been especially surprised by these accounts.

18

Hard Times Ahead

1 9 3 1 − 1 9 3 5

CMTC was still humming along in 1931 and 1932. Fifty-three camps were conducted in 1931 with 37,222 men completing; a few hundred more were trained at 51 camps in 1932. One statistic, however, changed dramatically; the number of applications in 1931 increased almost 26 percent from the year before, and jumped another 19.5 percent in 1932 when the number of applications hit a new high of almost 100,000.[1] As much as the War Department and the MTCA might have wished to attribute the increases to continued improvements in recruiting, the surge in the program's popularity was more likely the result of the nation's worsening economy.

Unemployment had reached either 4.8 million or 2.5 million, depending on whether one accepted the figure announced by William Green, president of the American Federation of Labor, or the lower figure claimed by President Hoover. Whatever the numbers, the economic situation was bad and getting worse. Some 2,300 of the nation's banks had failed since 1929, sales were falling—even for bootleg whiskey—and consumer prices sagged as money became harder to come by.[2]

A month at summer camp—with three square meals a day, clean clothes, a little cash to warm the pockets, good fellowship, and plenty to keep a young guy busy—was a deal that was hard to beat in the 1930s. Had the appropriation money been available, there is little doubt that President Harding's dream of 100,000 candidates a year could have been reached and sustained.

CMTC had escaped Congress's economic scalpel through 1932, but the War Department saw what was coming. The Democrat-controlled House's subcommittee on War Department appropriations was set to perform some radical surgery with its draft of the 1933 fiscal year appropriations bill (which would fund the 1932 camps). It proposed to cut 10,000 of the Army's 130,000 men, drastically curtail the already anemic Officers' Reserve Corps program, and suspend CMTC for at least one year. The War Department avoided, for that year at least, the cuts proposed by the subcommittee, managing to fully retain the CMTC program for 1932.[3] But the surgery wasn't canceled, it was only postponed.

As tough as times were there still was a presidential election to be held in 1932. President Hoover was renominated by the Republicans and Franklin Delano Roosevelt, a former Secretary of the Navy and recently governor of New York, was the Democrats' choice. Roosevelt not only won in the November election, as expected, but scored a landslide victory, winning all but 6 of the 48 states. The lame-duck Hoover administration's proposed budget for the 1934 fiscal year cut CMTC's funding in half—down to a lean $1 million. In what some members may have considered a "mercy killing," the House Appropriations committee elected to abolish CMTC. The *New York Times* reported the committee as saying that it eliminated all appropriations for CMTC "because the budget had recommended, as compared with $2,603,624 available this year [for the 1933 camps], only $1,000,000, which would reduce the trainees from 37,500 to 13,000. This, the committee said, would not only bar any new enrolments [*sic*], but also exclude nearly half of those who have passed the initial or basic course."[4] Ultimately Congress restored the $1 million, and the War Department rejected the option of committing euthanasia and chose instead what surely would be a slow death for CMTC. For the summer of 1933, with its former quota of 35,000 cut in half, the War Department made the decision to accept no first-year candidates.[5] If that practice were to continue for three or four more years CMTC would die at its roots.

The Army's inability to accept new applicants, or even some of those with past CMTC training, had no immediate dampening effect on the flow of applications. A new record for the number of applications—106,834—was received in 1933.[6] Roscoe Norman was one of the many thousands of young men who were disappointed that summer. He had been accepted for his first year but was later told of the cancellation of the Basic course. Norman persisted and was accepted for the 1934 course at Fort Benjamin Harrison, in spite of the War Department's CMTC appropriation being increased by a measly $5,394. Records don't reveal how the Army managed to offer all four years that summer, when the quota for the year was even smaller than for 1933; not quite reaching 17,000. The word was getting out, however, about the slow strangulation of the program, and 1934 applications fell to not quite 45,000.[7]

That the number of scheduled camps remained almost the same in both 1933 and 1934 as in past years defies explanation. Forty-nine camps were conducted in 1933 and 48 in 1934, although less than half the usual number of candidates attended.[8]

One CMTC alumnus expressed the belief that Roosevelt's creation of the Civilian Conservation Corps (CCC) in 1933, which paid its young members $30 a month (more than Army privates made at the time), was the cause of CMTC's drastic drop in attendance in 1933 and 1934. As logical as this reasoning may seem, the War Department's reported figures don't support the theory. It is evident there were enough young Americans at loose ends during this dismal time to have filled large quotas for all the armed services, as well as CMTC and CCC.

★

With CMTC having survived, albeit barely, a young man selected as one of the 15,000 men to attend CMTC in 1933 could consider himself fortunate. In July a group of CMTC candidates at Fort Myer, Virginia, near Washington, D.C., must have felt

Col. Harry Truman, Officers' Reserve Corps, was a CMTC commander at Camp Pike, Arkansas, for two weeks in 1933, the year before he entered the United States Senate. Here the future president is shown at Fort Riley, Kansas, while performing annual active duty in July 1926. His fellow officer is identified as Capt. Hurd, Field Artillery Reserve. (The Harry S. Truman Library.)

doubly fortunate when they were chosen to visit the White House and meet two of the nation's most famous men. The mansion had a new occupant, Franklin D. Roosevelt, who was unquestionably the country's "Man of the Hour." The President's busy schedule called for him to meet the CMTC contingent and, at the same time, greet the famous aviator Wiley Post. Post, who wore a distinctive white patch to cover a defective left eye, had just completed a record-setting flight around the world with navigator Harold Gatty. The newspaper account reported that after Roosevelt welcomed Post and his wife, the President invited the Posts to join him while he addressed the military group.

Roosevelt told the Fort Myer candidates that he wished he had "the time and opportunity of going to see you in camp," and added that he also wished he had been young enough to have "partaken of the chance of going to the training camps." (Certainly no one dared mention to the President that in 1915 he was of an age to have attended the Plattsburg camps, as had so many Easterners of his class.) When Roosevelt invited Post to address the CMTC group and the radio audience, the aviator told the candidates, "I admire the American uniform a great deal. I am sorry I have never worn it."[9]

★

Material submitted by CMTC alumni has revealed several people with direct CMTC connections in the 1930s who later would attain varying degrees of prominence. Heading the list were two future presidents.

Richard Corbyn, who attended his third year at Camp Pike, Arkansas, said his CMTC commander for the last two weeks of camp was Army Reserve Col. Harry Truman. Special Orders No. 76, dated July 17, 1933, issued by the 102nd Division, Saint Louis, Missouri, did, indeed, direct that Harry S Truman was to report to Camp Pike on August 17, 1933, for 14 days active duty.[10]

Former President Ronald Reagan has written of his mid-1930 CMTC experience: "[An] announcer at WHO, a reserve officer in the army cavalry, told me the Fourteenth Cavalry Regiment at Fort Des Moines [Iowa] offered young men a chance to obtain a reserve commission through what the War Department called the Citizens' Military Training Program [sic]. I didn't have a burning desire to be an army officer. I still thought we'd fought the war to end all wars—but it was a deal too good to turn down.* In exchange for enlisting in the reserve, the army offered training by some of the best cavalrymen in the country and unlimited use of army horses, all free."[11] In 1968 the future president of the United States said that earning a reserve commission was "one of the smartest things I ever did."[12]

---

*In *Early Reagan,* by Ann Edwards (see note 12), the writer seems to establish the date of his commission in the "Reserve Cavalry [sic]" as 1936, after having trained at "Camp Dodge." It appears the writer has confused Camp Dodge, an historical but inactive post, with Fort Des Moines, an active post at that time.

Former President Ronald Reagan, while working as an announcer for radio station WHO in the 1930s, signed up for cavalry training at Fort Des Moines, Iowa, where he earned a commission in the Organized Reserve Corps. He later called this service "one of the smartest things I ever did." (The U.S. Horse Cavalry Association, Fort Riley, Kansas.)

P. L. Wells said that when he and his brother attended their third year in 1931 at Camp Beauregard, Louisiana, a friend of theirs, Paul ("Bear") Bryant, was also enrolled. Bryant left camp before completing, Wells said, to enroll in the University of Alabama, where he and legendary football player Don Hutson held down the flanks of the Crimson Tide line. Bryant went on to become a legend in his own right as the nation's winningest college football coach, guiding the teams of Alabama and, earlier, the University of Kentucky and Texas A & M.

In 1931 and 1932 the commander of the Presidio of Monterey and each of the summers' CMTC was Col. Ben Lear.[13] In 1941, as a lieutenant general, Lear gained a prominence—nigh on to notoriety—that, unhappily for him, went well beyond any fame provided by his three stars. As a result of taking stern disciplinary action against a convoy of troops who yelled "yoo-hoo" at young women on the grounds of a Memphis country club, he earned the public's scorn and the ire of Congress, and was awarded the humiliating nickname, "Yoo-Hoo General" Ben Lear.[14]

Jean Lambert contributed a photocopy of the Military Training Certificate from his fourth year at Fort Snelling in 1934 signed by the camp assistant adjutant, 2d Lt. H. K. Johnson. Gen. Harold K. Johnson was Chief of Staff of the Army in the late 1960s at the height of the Vietnam War.

★

In the early 1930s aviation was coming of age, with a variety of flying records and first-time aerial accomplishments being set. In 1932 aviatrix (the term of the time) Amelia Earhart became the first woman to make a solo flight across the Atlantic, flying nonstop from Newfoundland to Ireland in 14 hours, 50 minutes.

Unfortunately, with the advances in aviation also came trage-dies. Knute Rockne, who coached Notre Dame from football obscurity to national fame, died in 1931 with seven others in the crash of a tri-motored Fokker in a Kansas field. The U.S. Navy's "Akron," the world's largest dirigible when it carried 207 passen-gers on its 1931, 10-hour maiden flight, crashed in an April 1933 storm on the East Coast. Seventy-three of its 77-member crew drowned.

A family tragedy involving the world's most renowned aviator, Charles Lindbergh, brought additional gloom to a nation mired in the Depression. The Lindberghs' year-and-a-half-old son was kidnapped on March 2, 1932. Two months later the baby's body was found in a bush by a roadway about five miles from the Lindberghs' home. Events connected to the horrible event re-mained in the news and the public consciousness for the rest of the decade.

★

Was it the result of powerful lobbying, some improvement in the economy, a new feeling of hope generated by Roosevelt's New Deal, or the frightening developments in Europe and Asia that caused Congress to become less miserly with defense appropriations for fiscal year 1936? Whatever the reason, the new generosity resulted in CMTC being appropriated $2 million for the 1935 camps. A quota of nearly 34,000 was established, and 30,084 young men were trained at 49 camps, with almost 54,000 applying.[15]

On August 16, 1935, radios across the nation announced that Will Rogers and Wiley Post were killed instantly when their plane plummeted into a frozen riverbank while touring Alaska. Humorist Rogers epitomized the cliché of the day, "star of stage, screen, and radio." He also was beloved as a political satirist through his syndicated newspaper column and radio appearances, even gaining the affection of his targets. Will Rogers's death was mourned by the entire nation, including CMTC candidates. That summer some of them might have paid their 10-cents post theater admission to see Rogers's 1934 movie *Judge Priest* or one of his earlier movies, including an outlandish adaptation of Mark Twain's *A Connecticut Yankee in King Arthur's Court.* *

Leland Cubbage still remembered a notorious event in 1934 that happened in nearby Chicago when he was in CMTC training at Fort Sheridan. He was walking guard on the night in late July that FBI Agent Melvin Purvis and his fellow G-men fatally shot John Dillinger, dubbed Public Enemy #1, outside a Chicago movie house. The conditions of the day had created a fertile breeding ground for gangsters and other famous hoodlums, many as well publicized as movie stars. That year—1934—turned out to be a bad one for several other infamous bandits. The Texas Rangers bushwacked Clyde Barrow and Bonnie Parker (forever-

---

*I was a seven-year-old living in a small town in Kentucky that summer in 1935. My beloved maternal grandmother (who lived in Madisonville) was visiting us when the news came over the radio. That afternoon when I came in from play my grandmother's sobbing was so near hysteria that I thought there must have been a death in the family. She was sobbing over the death of her favorite movie comedian with the same intensity she often had shown in her almost hysterical laughter at Rogers's on-screen antics (sometimes to the embarrassment of a seven-year-old).

more known as Bonnie and Clyde) on a deserted road outside Shreveport, Louisiana. In October Melvin Purvis increased his fame by being one of several lawmen who gunned down Charles ("Pretty Boy") Floyd. The next month in Chicago two federal agents shot it out with George ("Baby Face") Nelson, who got away but was found dead the next day in a ditch outside the city with 17 bullets in his body. The year had barely ended when on January 16, 1935, a dozen or more G-men cut down Kate ("Ma") Barker and her son Fred, both long-sought members of the Karpis gang. The agents cornered the Barkers in their Florida hideout and killed them after a six-hour gun battle.

By the mid-1930s, boys who in just a few years would be eligible to join CMTC could already belong to Melvin Purvis' "Junior G-man" club by saving box tops from Post Toasties® corn flakes. The makers of the popular cereal gave Purvis, recently retired, a chance to cash in on his fame as a G-man, providing American boys with an impressive tin badge and fantasy adventures.*

Children, youths, and adults alike could indulge their fantasies and escape the harsh realities of the day by going to the movies or, even less costly, by turning on the radio. The movies playing in 1935 offered adventure—*China Seas* with Clark Gable, Jean Harlow, and Wallace Beery; family fun—*Curly Top* starring Shirley Temple; or romance—*Anna Karenina* starring the mysteriously beautiful Greta Garbo. Radio was blossoming with a wide variety of new programs, some attempting to challenge the popularity of "Amos 'n' Andy," the black-face pair who had dominated the airwaves since 1928. "One Man's Family," the long-running "soap opera," which unlike most of the "soaps" was broadcast in the evenings, began in 1932. "Fibber McGee and Molly," a radio situation comedy, was introduced in 1935. Another comedy pair,

---

*During this period I was a loyal Post Toasties® eater and each year faithfully renewed my Junior G-man membership.

"Lum and Abner" began a 24-year run, spending some time on each of the four radio networks.

By the end of 1935 the Great Depression was still around, but things were beginning to look up, if only slightly. Citizens' Military Training Camps had not only survived but had begun to revive. Through the remainder of the 1930s CMTC would continue to regain strength in what was to be its final quarter of life.

★ 19 ★

Earning the Gold Bar

In spite of CMTC's public acceptance and its increasingly successful recruiting efforts, attrition remained endemic to the program. Young Americans who were accepted for the Basic year could look forward to the prospect of completing three more years and "grabbing the brass ring," which in this case was the gold bar of an Army second lieutenant. In reality, however, throughout the program's 20 years only an average of about six percent of Basic candidates completed the fourth, or Blue year. For an example, there were 500 Basic CMTC candidates in the 1934 camp at Fort Benjamin Harrison. "Four years later five of us were commissioned second lieutenants, for a rate of one percent," recalled Roscoe Norman. In 1927, for the first and only time in CMTC's 20-year history, the War Department published a breakdown of the number completing all four courses during the summer of 1927: Of the 38,597 who completed CMTC in 1927, 25,179 were Basics; 8,372 were White; 3,359 were Red; and only 1,696 were graduating Blues.[1]

But being a graduate of the Blue course wasn't tantamount to gaining the gold bar, at least after 1925. The War Department in 1923 reported 348 CMTC graduates having been commissioned, probably the first group to earn the bar through the fledgling program. In 1924, 501 were commissioned and 299 became second lieutenants in 1925.[2] During those early years commissions may have been tendered to Blue course graduates with merely a favorable recommendation from the camp commander and a successful interview by a board of officers. Apparently there was no requirement to complete a pre-commissioning correspondence course, known for years as the Army's 10-Series sub-course.

Standards for commissioning had tightened up considerably by 1927. The War Department's 1928 Annual Report, listing only 23 commissions in 1927, explained that "regulations require service of at least one year in the regular Army, the National Guard, or the Organized Reserves, and satisfactory completion of the prescribed course of study [which, at least in later years, was the 10-Series] before a commission will be given."[3] The unpopular policy lasted less than three years. During fiscal year 1930 the War Department amended the regulation and only required Blue course graduates desiring a commission to be members of the Regular Army, the National Guard, or the Organized Reserves *at the time of appointment*. The War Department felt the change in Army Regulations "should result in a material increase in the number of graduates commissioned in the Reserve Corps."[4] Ultimately it did. After the measly 23 commissions awarded in 1927 only 30 were reported for 1928 and 46 in 1929. In 1930 the number more than doubled to 114, still a pitifully small number considering those 2,037 who graduated from the Blue course that year. By 1931 the commissions had increased to 325, a number that would remain about average for each of CMTC's final 10 years.[5]

If the War Department's yearly figures on commissions awarded during the 20 years of CMTC are taken at face value, the program appears to have failed as a source of second lieutenants for the Organized Reserve Corps. According to the Army's reported numbers, slightly more than 5,000 CMTC graduates were appointed second lieutenants during that program's 20 years.[6] In any year, even a bad one, during that same period, the ROTC commissioned more than 5,000 college graduates. The 5,000 CMTC commissioning figure when compared with the estimated total of 370,000 young men who attended at least one year of CMTC shows those gaining a commission to have been only 1.35 percent—a figure strikingly close to Roscoe Norman's experience.* But perhaps CMTC's contribution to the Officers' Reserve Corps was better than the numbers would indicate. The War Department's statistics may not have been the third type of lie (according to Mark Twain, Benjamin Disraeli said that the three types of lies were "lies, damned lies, and statistics"[7]) but they were inclined to be incomplete. In its final report on CMTC the War Department acknowledged its commissioning figures for CMTC "are subject to change, as appointments are accepted by graduates who received certificates entitling them to appointment within 5 years from date of graduation."[8]

The men who contributed their CMTC experiences to this book have the distinction of representing all 20 years of the program. Of the 184 who responded to the author's questionnaire, 41 of them—22 percent—gained their commissions through CMTC as compared with the estimated 1.35 percent commissioned during the program's entirety. The apparent statistical aberration can be explained by the fact that those in the contributor group were located through items in military-oriented publications; the majority of the group having gone on to pursue active duty or reserve military careers.

The oral history contributed by the group of 184 provides strong evidence that the CMTC experience influenced a significant, although undocumented, number of young men to later seek

---

*Let's Pull Together for the C.M.T.C., a pamphlet published in 1938, reported 307,317 individual young men having attended at least one year of CMTC by 1937. The next year the New York Times (March 19, 1939, Sect. III, p. 5) listed the number as 327,586 through 1938. Comparing these numbers with the total attendance for each of the years involved, it appears that about 60 percent of each year's total attendance consisted of first-time attendees. Applying this percentage to the total attendance for the final two years and adding it to the number of first-time attendees through 1938, it appears that an estimated 370,000 young Americans attended CMTC for at least one year during the program's 20 years.

and win commissions. Seven members of the group went on to graduate from military academies; five from West Point and two from the Naval Academy. Others attended college where they were commissioned through ROTC or completed OCS during World War II. It seems reasonable to believe this pattern may have applied to a vast number of CMTC alumni.

Marco Thorne said completing correspondence courses was out of the question as he pursued a bachelor's and master's degree in history from Stanford and later another graduate degree in librarianship from the University of California at Berkeley. Thorne, drafted in 1942 into the Army Air Force, applied for the Air Force's administrative Officer Candidate School. He said that after passing the written exam he was interviewed by two colonels "who were not impressed with the fact that I was a librarian (what kind of a he-man job is that, ha-ha!). I was rejected, saluted and was going out of the door when I was called back into the room. . . . 'You went to CMTC?' 'Yes sir.' 'Four years?' 'You were paid?' 'No sir. Only transportation expenses.' 'You gave your time to Uncle Sam for free for four summers?' 'Yes sir.' Silence. The two colonels looked at each other. Then the one with my papers said, 'If you were so patriotic then you deserve to go to OCS.' And so I did." Thorne was awarded his gold bar in October 1942 along with classmate Clark Gable at the Air Force's Administrative Officers' School in Miami Beach.

An appearance before a board of officers can make a lasting impression on a young person. Robert Miller, who was a Regular Army private, attended CMTC later in the 1930s at the Presidio of Monterey, skipping the Basic year as did most men with some previous military experience. His pre-commissioning board in Los Angeles gave him an oral exam with a hypothetical leadership problem to work: He is a platoon leader whose troops are to guard a water reservoir above Los Angeles. A trailer is set up by a group of prostitutes near there and he—the platoon leader—is to give the platoon a lecture on the dangers of VD. "So I started out like a normal lieutenant would do and gave some standard reasons not to visit that whorehouse. Then I remembered a lesson given by a Regular Army captain of Co. D, 30th Infantry Regiment, at one of my CMTCs where he ended with this story: A cat was playing beside a railroad track, a train came by and cut off his tail. The cat turned around to see what had happened and the train then cut off his head. The moral of the story is 'never lose your head over a piece of tail.' Well my pre-commission exam was cut short and I only had a couple of more questions. I'm sure that was because I used that story."

Few probably had as casual, and yet incisive, an appearance before a commissioning board as did Robert Wentworth after completing CMTC. His board convened at Boston Army Base in 1932. "The officers swore each other in, greeted me cordially, then disbanded to 'meet later.'" Wentworth said. "I was advised to check my records with the chief clerk, a civilian. He seemed like a friendly person, wanting to talk about anything that interested me—my college courses, my family, etc. It must have been at least two hours later that I discreetly inquired about when he thought the board would be ready to see me. 'You may go any time. I am a reserve officer. You have just had your examination!' he said."

A pre-commissioning board examining graduates of the 1927 Fort Du Pont CMTC may have found itself interviewing the most "overqualified" officer candidate in the program's history. Frank Stadler completed the Blue course "eligible for a commission in the Officers Reserve," according to the *New York Times*. The 29-year-old Stadler had begun his training four years earlier at Plattsburg Barracks. As a veteran of the World War, it appears he should have skipped the Basic year, and possibly even the Red course. But maybe the Army didn't consider Stadler's World War service to have qualified him as a veteran since he fought on the other side. A native of Hungary, he was a 16-year-old college student in Cologne when the war broke out. He immediately enlisted in the German Army and spent four years fighting the Russians, Rumanians, French, and British. At age 19 he was made a second lieutenant in the German 26th Trier Regiment. Stadler came to the U.S. in 1920 and became an American citizen.[9] What happened with his military future is lost to history, but based on his military past a strong case could have been made to appoint this former German Army second lieutenant a *first* lieutenant.

The widespread practice of accepting underage youths in the program was a cause of delay, or sometimes failure, in granting some commissions, because after finishing four years many lads were still two to three years away from 21, the minimum age for commissioning. Joseph Brennan completed his training at Camp Meade in 1939 but didn't receive his CMTC-earned gold bars until 1943. Robert Sumner, an alumnus of Vancouver Barrack's 1940 CMTC, qualified for a commission but wasn't awarded it until 1942, when the minimum age was lowered to 20.

★

CMTC's high attrition rate shouldn't be especially surprising. After all, it was a volunteer program aimed at young men in their formative years. Even for a young man who finished the Basic course and enthusiastically vowed to return for the second year, many a thing might change his mind in 12 months. A new job or a new girlfriend or hundreds of other less important matters might keep him from showing up for his Red year. Some who did take the second year and wished to return as White candidates weren't allowed to return because in the Army's opinion they didn't measure up. The Army continued tightening the standards as a candidate moved into the advanced year. Fifth Corps Area stated the criteria for being accepted for the final year: "At the end of the White Course all trainees not considered officer material will be eliminated from further advancement until fully qualified. Mere attendance at a White Course does not entitle a trainee to attend a Blue Course. No trainee will be admitted to the Blue

Course who does not have both the educational and physical requirements for commission in the Officers' Reserve Corps."[10]

Of course it took a large amount of motivation to become a Blue candidate and satisfy all the requirements for a commission. An article from a CMTC newspaper provided this guidance: "It has been suggested that White trainees who wish to earn commissions as second lieutenants, Organized Reserves, should prepare themselves before they enter their Blue year.

"They may enlist in the Enlisted Reserve Corps and will be assigned to their local regiment. The Unit Instructors of that Regiment will allow them to take the 10-series of sub-courses, which, with the completion of the blue course and a favorable recommendation of the examining board at the CMTC, will entitle them to a commission as 2nd Lt. in their branch of the Organized Reserves."[11]

For those few who did stick it out for four years the pinning on of the gold bar seemed worth the extra study required and any inconvenience caused by the four weeks of training each summer. The commissioning ceremony is one of life's events, which remains etched in the memory. For Dr. William Snell, an alumnus of the final camps at Vancouver Barracks, his commissioning was extraordinarily unforgettable. His gold bar was pinned on by an officer who stood at the threshold of immortality as a soldier-statesman—George C. Marshall. At the time, Marshall was commander of Vancouver Barracks. "My memory is distinct about him. An impressively brilliant officer who was at the same moment gentle and warm to a 'shavetail'—and a reservist to boot," Snell recalled.

The Several Sides of
Life at Camp

It wasn't just the training, the sports, and the off-duty time that filled the hours and clung to the memories of those who took the Army up on its offer of 30 days of summertime soldiering. The life of a soldier, even a part-time one, is made up of more elements than the non-military person probably could ever imagine. A candidate often found his environment and living conditions providing new experiences, and, frequently, challenges, as illustrated by Eugene Small's anecdote: "There were several permanent buildings at camp headquarters left over from World War I [Camp Dix, 1937], but we were housed in a regimental-size tent city. At the head of each company street was a permanent mess hall and latrine. An elevated road surrounded the tent city—a disaster when a cloud burst dammed up the culverts and we watched our shoes float out of the tents. Spent the next day locating the flotsam and digging out."

The flood Small remembered might have been from the same New Jersey summer cloudburst Elmer Froewiss recalled: "One evening (after a hard rain) we arrived to find all the mess halls flooded with about a foot of water. The mess halls were set in a hollow and a culvert was plugged, I believe. All hands turned to in bailing them out, and supper that night was delayed and consisted of sandwiches."

Ed Randall had a special memory of his company street at Fort

Brady, Michigan, and the GI-can urinals at the foot of the street: "Ever try to hit one at 3 A.M. when the cans were higher than you were?"

Of course, every candidate was an expert at one regular activity—eating. Regarding the often controversial subject of food—its preparation, its portions, and its consumption—the memories gathered for this book were almost unanimously favorable toward Army fare. The single negative opinion of the food came from Bud Rubel regarding the chow at Fort McClellan in the late 1930s. "I've always been a big eater but the food in the mess hall was fit for pigs," he declared.

A reserve captain serving as assistant mess officer submitted the following "after-action report" to a camp yearbook: "Since this article on the subject of the mess is more or less statistical, it will be well to state at the outset that there are approximately the following number of opinions from the following sources:

2,566 opinions from CMTC students

138 opinions from officers

90 opinions from mess sergeants and cooks

"The opinions vary from day to day and even from meal to meal. If frankfurters or saur kraut [sic] is served opinions differ, but they were quite unanimous upon the occasion of the Sunday dinner of August 20th, when the following menu was served:

Chicken Fricassee	Dumplings	Mashed Potatoes
Salad	Ice Cream	Apple Pie
Bread and Butter	Jelly	Lemonade

"The problem of feeding over 2,500 hungry young Americans for 30 days (a total of about a quarter of a million meals), keeping them filled and satisfied upon seventy cents a day per man was one of the big problems of the camp, for the Commanding Officer realized that the recollections of the camp would be largely influenced by whether or not their 'chow' was satisfactory."[1]

Although this book's contributors were almost unanimous in

Peeling spuds is just one of the many duties of a K.P., but was a favorite one of CMTC yearbook photographers. Chances are as soon as this photo was snapped most of this K.P. crew returned to scrubbing pots and pans, cleaning the garbage racks, or bringing in coal for the kitchen ranges. (Photo from the 1922 Camp Knox CMTC yearbook, The Mess Kit.*)*

their favorable memories of the food, the victuals served in Army messes weren't savored by everyone. John Gordon remembered being on guard duty at Fort Dix in 1940 when a CMTC company from Puerto Rico came close to mutiny over the chow. The year before, at the Presidio of Monterey, several advanced-year candidates tried to organize a mess hall walkout to demonstrate against the food. Camp officials took exception to the candidates' method of protest and after an investigation led by Lt. Col. James Van Fleet, executive officer for the camp, three of the instigators of the walkout were dismissed from camp and barred from further CMTC participation.[2] No record, however, was found showing what measures, if any, were taken to address the alleged mess problems. Van Fleet went on to face much tougher problems as a top commanding general in the European Theater during World War II, and as a four-star general and famous hero of the Korean War.[3]

The mess officer's article quoted earlier mentioned a 70-cent daily allowance for purchasing food. Although feeding young men, or anyone, for 70 cents a day is inconceivable today, in 1939 the daily rate was even less—only 60 cents for Regular Army soldiers—illustrating the price deflation caused by the Depression, which still lingered on. Despite Robert Sumner's impression that he and his fellow candidates at Vancouver Barracks in the late 1930s were allowed a ration and a half, there is evidence that at the time CMTC mess operations were allowed only a 10 percent increase over what was authorized for the Regular Army. Perhaps the rumbles over the chow at Monterey and the next year at Dix were the result of complaints over puny portions as much as gripes about poor preparation.

Granting the importance of food preparation, the adequate filling of young stomachs was the first consideration for Army mess sergeants and cooks. Candidates sometimes found they had to make adjustments in their food tastes in order to satisfy their youthful hunger. Paul Keough said his Basic year at Fort Devens was "my first introduction to food not prepared in standard New England cooking [method]." Marco Thorne said he and his fellow Jewish candidates at the Presidio of Monterey soon learned to "address pork as 'chicken.'" Perhaps pork chops were dubbed veal chops. Bacon would have been harder to fit with an alias, and may have been disdained by Jewish candidates in the hope that the next day's breakfast menu might offer "SOS" (an acronym for chipped beef on toast's scatological nickname).

Eating wasn't the candidates' only source of mess-hall experiences and memories. Mess sergeants and cooks often were unforgettable. Donald Armstrong remembered a particularly tough mess sergeant at Plattsburg in the early 1920s. Armstrong said during a visit to the mess hall, a general asked the man next to him how the food was. "Well, we had a real thug for a mess sergeant who would have slit throats for the slightest reason, so you can imagine the reply that the general got," Armstrong said. "This mess sergeant was really something. We were not allowed to talk or make any excess noise whatever in the mess hall while eating. We ate in absolute silence." Jean Lambert said the only tough noncommissioned officers he remembered were the ones who ran the mess halls. John Middlebrooks told of a ghastly incident while pulling K.P. at Fort Barrancas, Florida. A fellow K.P. reached for something a cook thought he shouldn't have. The cook, high on lemon extract, cut off one of the K.P.'s finger tips with a carving knife. The cook was court-martialed.

No other CMTC alumnus recounted a K.P. experience anywhere as gruesome. In fact, the memories generally ranged from the benign to the pleasant. The duty started early and ended late, but there were advantages also—more to eat and a break from the daily training routine. The original CMTC regulation stated that candidates were not to be used as kitchen police.[4] Later regulations mentioned no such prohibition. The Army may have begun detailing candidates to K.P. for several reasons. Permanent kitchen help, usually civilians, were a drain on funds, and there usually was a scarcity of Regular Army troops to pull the duty. A strong case also could have been made that K.P. was an important and traditional role of soldiering.

Pulling pranks was just as traditional as washing dishes or peeling spuds. Although he attended only one year, David Gray recalled his CMTC experiences vividly. He furnished this apt description of the protocol of pranks: "In the Army, then as part of the rights of passage, rookies were treated to a whole bag of tricks and pranks, partly of course to amuse the pranksters, but also to develop character in the prankee—a favorite one being the dispatch of a K.P. to another mess hall to borrow some exotic piece of equipment such as a sky hook or a gravy boat. After being passed from one mess hall to another the K.P. would realize he had been had, and so a lesson had been learned. The old-timers also loved a fight. If things got too quiet they weren't above instigating a row. A favorite trick was to fill a light bulb with ammonia and toss it into a barracks. When we came streaming out they were there to helpfully point out that they saw fellows from another barracks do the tossing. We of course took the bait and a grand melee generally ensued, with the regulars as enthusiastic spectators and to see that things didn't get out of hand, turning the fire hose on us on one occasion. However, we eventually realized we were being set up and so another lesson had been learned; more character had been built."

Bill Bentson remembered some of the standard barracks tricks and explained the psychology that sometimes motivated the pranksters: "Short-sheeting was prevalent the first week of camp and unknown to the newcomers. One night a sound sleeper was carried in his bunk with ease and finesse and left in the center of the company street. Another crawled into his cot one night and left same in great haste for someone had placed a garter snake in his sheets. Pranks were played on newcomers, cadet officers, and those who were susceptible to this type of treatment, due to their attitude, or psychological or physical makeup."

At camps where candidates were provided steel cots rather than folding canvas cots, energetic practical jokers would substitute string for the coil springs holding the metal mesh to the bed frame. Ned Wiencke and a buddy were two of those energetic pranksters. After altering the cot "we had not planned on the occupant sitting down just when the Officer of the Day entered the barracks. The entire barracks broke out into laughter as the candidate sat down and ended up on the floor with his legs draped over the side of the cot."

Two CMTC alumni who attended different camps in the mid-1930s witnessed similar bizarre incidents that qualify as unbelievably bone-headed stunts. "On a parade, after the regular sergeant told us to shine up our rifles, one CMTC member (he had to be First-year) took steel wool and shined all the bluing off his rifle and it shone like a silver dollar. He almost got court-martialed," recalled Arnold Silver. Although there was no authority to court-martial the erring candidate, the Army could have billed him the price of a Springfield. James Cantwell's anecdote from his training at Fort Sheridan is just as incongruous: "Showing up for reveille one morning we heard the sergeant yell 'what the hell did you do to your rifle? Come out here!' And then we were able to see the most beautiful silver rifle we had ever seen. He had 'Blitz-clothed' his '03. It took him all weekend to get the bluing off."

Rivalry between units often would inspire pranks, and the pranks might lead to combat. Bruce Romick said his Cavalry unit at Fort Des Moines had an active rivalry with the nearby Infantry company. "Occasionally, we'd be awakened by the sound of rocks hitting our tents," he remembered, "and in response a few rocks would find their way back to the Infantry area."

"Fights between cadets did occur and the solution was to put gloves on them and put them in the boxing ring during sports time," Bill Bentson recalled. "If this got too rough in a grudge fight, the officer would call the fight off and have them shake hands."

With considerable understatement Dr. Samuel Miller described as "a bad experience" an incident at Fort Custer, Michigan, in 1925: "I shared my tent with two young residents of [a suburb of Detroit] consisting of many young seriously anti-Semitic people [Miller is Jewish]. An early mutual dislike soon turned to a hateful environment, and slurring remarks eventually threatened physical violence. One day I heard a familiar click and turned to find myself facing a loaded rifle in the hands of one of these young men as he obviously cocked the weapon, pointing it at my chest and declaring that 'for two cents' he would pull the trigger. This was a serious violation of Army rules and surprisingly I took it quite calmly, reminding him of the violation. He lowered the gun and hinted that a fight with boxing gloves was in order. We were well matched physically and things went about equally until he butted my face with his head, fracturing my nose. This was the end of the match but hostilities continued for the duration, although on a lower hate level. I did not report the Army regulation violation concerning the threat with a cocked rifle loaded with live ammunition." (Unauthorized possession of live ammunition itself has always been a serious offense.)

None of the disputes and conflicts contributed by other CMTC alumni could in anyway match the intensity of Dr. Miller's. Most were resolved quickly not only with no hard feelings but often with an improved relationship. David Gray told of a barracks mate whose obnoxious bullying caused the rest of the platoon to physically throw him and his gear out in the company street. At the end of camp the culprit looked up Gray and "thanked me for kicking him out of the barracks; that it had made him realize what a jerk he had been and he would never forget it."

On the first night at Camp Knox, his hometown friend, Tony, "broke out a nightgown" at bedtime, Gray said. "I thought this meant trouble but didn't say anything. Sure enough several nights later a guy made some snide remark about it. Without saying a word Tony got out of bed and knocked the heckler flat on his ass. He then asked if there were any other comments and there were none."

For those young pranksters or belligerent candidates who felt the need of easing their conscience, Citizens' Military Training Camps seemed to always be well staffed with chaplains of all the major faiths. And, of course, church services were a scheduled event—mandatory at some camps and voluntary at others. At Camp Devens, Massachusetts, those attending the 1922 camp were advised: "Attendance at religious services is not compulsory, but students will be expected to observe the usual customs they practice at home."[5]

According to Alexander Borysewich attendance at Sunday services was virtually mandatory at Camp Dix: "On Sundays [1936] when Church Call was sounded we all had to fall in to go for church services. If not we would be put on details for various housekeeping duties. My company never did have a very clean house as we all were on the way to church."

Whether mandatory or not it seems the main means of transporting the troops to church was by marching: "In the Infantry at Fort Devens [1937, 1938] church was mandatory. The 13th Infantry band would be on hand as about 90 percent of the CMTC regiment marched off to Catholic Mass at the CMTC chapel. The other 10 percent, whether Lutheran, Episcopal, Baptist, Jewish, or atheist marched off to the Protestant services. I cannot remember any griping about it. It was one of the few occasions when we marched from point A to point B without a rifle on our shoulder," Paul Keough observed.

Not surprisingly the march favored by many Army bands for moving the candidates to church was "Onward Christian Soldiers." Who can say how much more mischief or pugnaciousness might have occurred the coming week if these volatile young men hadn't been given an opportunity to soothe the spirit?

Selling CMTC

1 9 2 1 – 1 9 4 0

In its 20-year life CMTC was blessed with a multitude of recruiting and publicity efforts provided by an eclectic array of organizations, alliances, and individuals. Although the other eight U.S. Army corps areas couldn't call on the powerful and loyal voice of the *New York Times* as could the Second Corps Area, CMTC steadily gained national recognition. After the program's first three years it always met its national quota, with applications to spare.

It surely was the interest shown at the grass-roots level that determined how successful a community was in selling the program to its young men. Clyde Boden said he was one of 60 lads from Shamokin, Pennsylvania, who attended CMTC in 1938. His hometown in rural Pennsylvania had a population of about 1,700 at the time.[1] On the other hand, Madisonville, Kentucky, a town in rural western Kentucky with four times the population of Shamokin, apparently did not come close to that number during the program's entire 20 years.* Community interest and organization, or its lack, is the obvious explanation for such a difference.

The word-of-mouth recommendation of a satisfied customer

---

*Although no CMTC recruiting figures for Madisonville are available, the author, who was reared there, located only two names of Madisonville men who attended CMTC and found few residents of the appropriate age who even recalled the program's existence. Madisonville's 1940 population was 8,209. (Associated Press news story, Dec. 31, 1940.)

always has been an effective sales tool. Earl ("Buck") Weaver, after two years of CMTC at Camp McCoy, Wisconsin, "sold all my friends on going to camp" in 1938, and brought along 17 of his buddies from Sheboygan.

Several CMTC alumni said their decision to sign up was influenced by older relatives or neighbors, often men with military experience. None of those mentors could have experienced sol-diering any farther back than did the man who persuaded Chandler Rudicel to attend CMTC at Fort Leavenworth in 1923. Rudicel's grandfather, a Civil War veteran, brought him a CMTC announcement from the local newspaper. Rudicel's reminiscence illustrates just how young this nation was in the 1920s.

As discussed in Chapter 3, recruiting in 1922 was less than successful. The poor showing of 1922 may have influenced sup-porters to intensify their publicity and public relations efforts the next year. In 1923 the *New York Times* ran four times the number of items about the camps than it had in 1922.[2] In 1923 the War Department began lobbying the legislature with letters signed by General Pershing, the Chief of Staff, inviting each of the nation's congressmen to visit one or more of the Army summer training camps (also including ROTC, National Guard, and Organized Reserve) in or near the congressman's constituency.[3] Corps area commanders were directed to follow up the Chief of Staff's invitation to arrange visits to specific locations.*

Second Corps Area devised a publicity stunt in 1922 worthy of a 20th-century Barnum. One July day Manhattan pedestrians

---

*In a letter to Hon. John F. Carew, Member of Congress, New York City, identical to the several hundred signed by General Pershing, the congressman is invited to observe any or all of the summer training scheduled—National Guard, Organized Reserve Corps, ROTC, and CMTC. Although many of the congress-man's responses on file at the National Archives were typically noncommittal, Congressman Carew—in longhand on the back of the original letter—responded positively. The Chief of Staff's letters to corps area commanders were classified "Confidential."

noticed that an airplane skywriting an advertisement for a popular cigarette began spelling out "Join CMTC." The skywritten message was described as five-miles long with three-quarter-mile-high letters. Regular Army recruiters and reserve officers in uniform were positioned on street corners around the city passing out leaflets, which explained the message to the curious public. The leaflets instructed those interested to visit the Army Building at 39 Whitehall Street in the city.[4] Unfortunately there is no record of how many showed up.

The War Department's initial CMTC regulation gave commanding generals of corps areas only the broadest guidance on how to publicize the program, directing that they "will cause to be prepared and distributed such circulars and subject matter of the information relative to the camps as they may deem necessary," and authorizing the commanders to pay for the materials with CMTC supply and services funds.[5] After its 1923 camps, Ninth Corps Area published a pamphlet with extracts of 16 letters to camp commanders from parents.[6] These "third-person" endorsements were intended as a key recruiting vehicle for the Ninth Corps Area in 1924. "A careful reading of the letters will convince any parent just what the Citizens' Military Training Camps are doing for our young men," the recruiting piece stated.

If any corps area commander doubted how committed General Pershing was to CMTC the doubt should have vanished after Pershing's letter to the Commanding General of First Corps Area.[7] In a three-page letter beginning "My dear General," the Chief of Staff admonished him for meeting only 75 percent of First Corps Area's quota, with but 85 percent of those who did apply reporting to camp. The letter pointed out that the First Corps Area's total attendance of 1,853 was about 60 percent of its allotted quota of 3,000—the lowest percentage of all corps areas. One corps area reached its full original quota and three recorded more than 90 percent. Pershing said that only two corps areas beside the First fell "materially below" 75 percent. Such a letter undoubtedly caught the First Corps Area commander's attention. In 1924 attendance at the two camps in First Corps Area increased by 900.[8]

Another general officer in 1923 learned in a painful way just how protective the War Department was in its role as the fledgling program's guardian. Brig. Gen. Dwight E. Aultman, commander of Fort Benjamin Harrison, Indiana, for 1922 and 1923 had also commanded Camp Knox during the inactive post's summer training period.[9] A strong supporter of the National Guard, Aultman was not sold on CMTC after observing the program for at least two years. He put these doubts on record to the Commanding General of Fifth Corps Area, recommending the abolishment of CMTC or converting it into a training program for National Guard recruits.[10] Although his recommendation had virtually no chance of being favorably considered by higher headquarters, he wouldn't have caught the devil for his devil's advocacy if he hadn't delivered much the same message before a meeting of the Indiana Reserve Officers' Association. Even then he might have avoided the wrath of the War Department if his comments hadn't been reported in the *Indianapolis News,* and particularly if his own post newspaper, *Fifth Corps News and Diamond Dust,* hadn't reprinted the item. The post newspaper somehow made its way to Maj. Gen. George B. Duncan, commander of Seventh Corps Area in Omaha, Nebraska. Duncan, a CMTC supporter, had recently received a batch of correspondence from the Missouri Adjutant General, who, along with several Missouri National Guard officers, had several bones to pick with CMTC. Gathering all these materials together Duncan wrote the Army Adjutant General saying, in part, "I feel that the War Department should be advised that criticism of the C.M.T. Camps is being fomented by National Guard officers in this Corps Area, especially in Missouri and Iowa. . . . In my opinion this opposition will be increased by utterances such as these attributed to General Aultman."[11]

The Adjutant General appeared to agree for he referred the matter to the Secretary of War, who directed that a letter be sent to Aultman. Its third and final paragraph read: "The Secretary of War is amazed that an officer of your grade and length of service should be so woefully lacking in that spirit of loyalty and cooperation which is essential to success in the military profession. He directs that you be informed that he considers your action in this connection most reprehensible and trusts that you will so conduct yourself in the future that he may again have confidence in receiving from you the loyal and willing support of his policies that he expects of all officers of the Army. A copy of this letter will be filed with your records." It is safe to assume that a second star was never added to Brig. Gen. Aultman's tunic.

Scattered evidence shows that opposition to CMTC was not universal for all National Guard commanders and units. In his correspondence to the Army Adjutant General, Maj. Gen. Duncan said that the Minnesota Adjutant General had requested to put the "Guard encampment the same place and time as the C.M.T.Camps, on the grounds that it has been so advantageous to their own recruitment." By 1923 the War Department was urging third-year men (White candidates) to join one of the Army's three components, a requirement for entering the Blue course. The War Department directive stated: "The candidates will be advised to enlist in the National Guard which is maintained in a more immediate state of readiness for active duty than the reserves. . . ."[12] The Fort Snelling yearbook for 1924 carried four National Guard recruiting ads: one from Arkansas, one from Iowa, and, amazingly, two ads from Missouri.[13] The Missouri Adjutant General must have thought it best to keep all his options open. Maj. Gen. William N. Haskell, commanding general of the New York National Guard, in 1926 spoke to the Brooklyn Rotary Club urging businessmen to cooperate with CMTC.[14] Had CMTC's attrition rate not been so high, it could have contributed significant numbers of recruits to the National Guard.

In 1928 the Secretary of War wrote: "Labor and capital have become a unit in the active encouragement of the camps. . . .

During the past four years a growing number of military schools, private schools, and colleges, among the latter many of the leading educational institutions in this country, have awarded scholarships bearing free tuition and other allowances to selected youths of the citizens' military training camps."[15] Yale University, at least in the 1930s, was one of those leading educational institutions:

"NEW HAVEN, Conn., April 4—Yale University today announced the offer of one scholarship each to a member of the 1933 First and Second Corps Area Citizens' Military Training Camps. The scholarships will amount to full tuition of $450 for the academic year 1933–1934. Competition is open to men who have fully qualified in June of this year for admission to Yale the following Fall."[16]

Several civilian organizations seemed to be competing with the Military Training Camps Association in its role, officially recognized by the War Department,[17] as the chief civilian supporter of CMTC. Among the most active were the Reserve Officers' Association (ROA), the Veterans of Foreign Wars (VFW), and the American Legion.[18] Examining some of the recorded actions of the VFW and the ROA, one might get the impression that each organization considered itself CMTC's principal advocate.[19] Perhaps there was a reasonable amount of coordination and cooperation between the groups since it is quite likely many active citizens were members of two or more of the organizations.

Support by national organizations wasn't limited to those with male-only membership. The 36th Congress of the National Society of the Daughters of the American Revolution passed a resolution praising CMTC.[20] Another strong supporter of CMTC was the National Patriotic Council, which according to its letterhead was "For Coordinated Patriotic Effort, Advocacy of Adequate National Defense and Opposition to Communism and Ultra-Pacifism." Each year, beginning in the early 1930s, the council presented gold medals to candidate-winners of essay contests.[21]

The War Department never wanted for sources of medals to

award to candidates. Among those local and national organizations offering military decorations none seemed more energetic than the VFW. In 1928 the VFW began awarding a medal to the top Basic candidate at each camp.[22] The organization produced extra publicity mileage by delivering the medals each year to the incumbent Army Chief of Staff. In 1932 the VFW's commander-in-chief presented 51 medals to Gen. Douglas MacArthur.[23] A War Department memorandum for the press confirmed the practice's continuation seven years later.[24]

MacArthur had been present at the creation of the "Plattsburg Movement" (see Chapter 1) and remained a strong supporter of CMTC through his tenure as Army Chief of Staff. During the appropriations battles with Congress in the early 1930s MacArthur defended CMTC to Congress as the "only program permitting sons of the poor to prepare for service."[25] As Third Corps Area commander, beginning in 1925, CMTC had been one of Mac-Arthur's major responsibilities—one he tackled enthusiastically according to biographer William Manchester. "Much of his time [as corps area commander] was spent as a glorified flack, huckstering ROTC and CMTC . . . programs—writing handouts, showing slides at Rotary and Kiwanis meetings, setting up movie newsreels on training camps, designing CMTC Christmas cards, and distributing in bus and train stations racks of leaflets extolling preparedness."[26]

The name of the first Army Chief of Staff connected with CMTC, General Pershing, was kept alive through the Pershing Medal, which was awarded in each of the nine corps areas to the person chosen the outstanding candidate for the year. Each winner was also treated to a free trip to Washington, D.C., where the medal was awarded by Black Jack Pershing himself.[27]

Before General Pershing retired as Chief of Staff he took an unusual step to promote CMTC. He wrote, or at least lent his byline to, a magazine article for the July 1924 issue of *Woman's Home Companion*.[28] In about 2,700 words—words that later in the 20th Century would be considered patronizing and sexist—he appealed to the patriotism of "American girls and women" to support the Organized Reserve and, specifically, the CMTC. "When it is understood that the women of America expect their men to prepare themselves for the defense of the country, there is no force that can hold them back. . . . The girl who reads the WOMAN'S HOME COMPANION would not marry an utterly uneducated man, or one unversed in the usages of decent society. Why should she not add to her list of ineligibles the man who is unequipped as a citizen, since he is untrained in a citizen's basic duty, the defense of his native land?" Concluding the article the general wrote: "When she supports citizen training as a reasonable measure of preparedness against the calamity of war, and as a great national school for better citizenship in time of peace, the success of this new adventure in democracy is assured. Here lies the American woman's supreme opportunity for patriotic service to-day [*sic*]."

The most famous supporter of CMTC had no military or particular patriotic credentials. George Herman ("Babe") Ruth, who had ensured his baseball immortality by hitting 60 home runs in 1927, was persuaded to lend his endorsement to CMTC. Maxwell Hamilton recalled a placard in a store window: "Featuring an enlarged photo of the great Babe Ruth in the midst of his typical home run swing, the poster carried a quote from the Bambino which said: 'If *I* had a son, I'd want him to attend a Citizens' Military Training Camp!'"[29] Ruth also agreed to autograph a baseball and bat as an award to the outstanding soldier athlete at each camp. It was a practice he continued at least through 1934 when he presented the Secretary of War with 48 baseballs and bats.[30] How many of these almost-priceless collectibles might be lying, still undiscovered, in attics around the nation? William Moher, of Nashua, New Hampshire, is sure at least one set of the autographed bats and balls is still around. He won the coveted prize by being voted the top baseball player at Fort Ethan Allen in the mid-1930s. He said his son has the bat and hoped that a nephew to whom Moher had given the ball has held on to it.

Maxwell Hamilton's inspiration for titling his article on CMTC "Some Called Us Cannon Fodder" was the special attention he and his fellow Plattsburg-bound passengers received that summer of 1927 from two young men:[31] "A couple of pseudo-newsboys entered the car and began handing out leaflets to everyone. These carried a message that was terse and to the point.

"'You're all FOOLS!' it said. . . . 'Can't you see you're being exploited by the Wall Street Capitalists and Munitions Makers! They plan to use you for nothing but CANNON FODDER! Come on—it's not too late! Join the People's Party of the Proletariat, and fight for freedom and justice!!'"* The two "newsboys" might have been among the three members of the Young Workers' League of America who were detained briefly the previous summer by the New York Central Railroad police for passing out pamphlets headed "CAMPS BREED WAR" to men headed for Plattsburg.[32]

The "Red Scare" of the early 1920s[33] may have abated somewhat but communism remained a bugbear for many Americans. In 1928 the VFW expressed the belief that "Bolshevism is slowly, but surely, finding its way into the life of the country."[34] In the same report the writer attributed a reduction of almost 700 youths reporting to CMTC camps in an unnamed corps area to the Young Workers Communist League who had "circularized to the men ordered to camp subversive literature asserting that the training was designed for the purpose of creating 'gun fodder' for capitalists' wars."[35]

The communist pamphleteers struck early in 1928, plastering six- by eight-inch leaflets on and around the Connecticut State

---

*Hamilton was headed for the first Plattsburg camp of the summer, opening July 2. Three members of the Young Workers were back at the Grand Central Station in August passing out their literature for the men headed for the August Plattsburg camp. According to the *New York Times* the three young men "from 18 to 20 years old were ordered from the Grand Central Terminal by members of the bomb squad." (August 7, 1927, p. 11.)

Capitol. The Hartford Communist Party took credit for the April 13 paper attack. Quoted in the *New York Times,* they denounced "citizens' military training camps as makers of 'cannon fodder' . . . calling the Federal Government and the industrial corporations of the nation 'conspirators' in the 'most imperialistic country in the world.'"[36]

Anti-CMTC activities by avowed communists weren't limited to the East Coast. Pat Herst remembered an episode at Vancouver Barracks in 1929 or 1930: "One exciting evening at a dance was the time a half-dozen or so teenagers from Portland came representing the communists. There would have been a brawl but officers made the pinkies go home." A near brawl wasn't the half of it in the Midwest one August evening in 1929. The *New York Times* reported:

"MINNEAPOLIS, Minn., Aug. 21—One thousand members of the Citizens Military Training Camp at Fort Snelling broke up a communistic meeting in Bride Square here last night and kidnapped one of the leaders.

"Raiding of the meeting followed distribution of Red propaganda among the cadets yesterday morning.

"Thomas Folay, a Communist organizer, was carried about a mile before his captors were overtaken by the police and their victim was freed.

"The cadets were returned to their camp in care of their company commanders, and were to be dealt with under army discipline."[37]

No follow-up story reported what disciplinary measures were taken, but a good guess would be the punishment consisted of nothing much more than a stern lecture by the commanding officer, who may have had trouble keeping a straight face.

When the 1930 CMTC at Camp Dix found itself papered with hundreds of pieces of communist literature one July morning the camp commander, Col. W. B. Graham, "professing himself to be undisturbed by the pamphlets" put the matter in proper context:

The U.S. Postal Department in the 1920s lent its support to CMTC recruiting by providing "slogan cancels," as they are called in philatelic circles.

"We are training these boys in citizenship, and if their loyalty couldn't stand exposure to the ravings of a few half-baked failures in life it would be a pretty sad reflection on the training. Naturally we would not tolerate any open soap-box activities in the camp—merely as a matter of discipline. But if these clowns get any thrill out of sneaking around in the dark and scattering the propaganda they're welcome to it. Any overt acts will be dealt with according to the law, however."[38]

The last incident of anti-CMTC propaganda found in newspaper accounts was in 1933 at Plattsburg Barracks where a mimeographed newspaper called "The Plattsburg Voice" was mailed to many of the candidates. In addition to attacking the Roosevelt administration and "militarism" the anonymous writer referred to the candidates as "servile cannon fodder and loyal slaves for the next war."[39]

Fear about dissident activities and publications hurting the CMTC program is difficult to support. It seems more likely that these inept efforts by fringe groups presented CMTC with one more source, among its many, of publicizing the program.

A War Department Slight,
Only Slightly Remedied
1 9 3 6 – 1 9 4 0

Finally, after 15 years, the War Department in 1936 made a move to accommodate African-American men who wanted to attend CMTC.* From the earliest days of the program the government appears to have consistently dissimulated regarding CMTC training available for young Negro men. Never in 20 years of annual reports did any Secretary of War delineate any policy on or even make any mention of CMTC training for African Americans. The matter first surfaced publicly in 1923, when the NAACP took the War Department to task for rejecting the application of a black youth from New Jersey.

The NAACP wasn't alone in criticizing the War Department for practicing racial discrimination in its management of CMTC. One of the civilian aides to the Secretary of War, all of whom, by

---

*War Department correspondence available in the National Archives on CMTC does not provide a comprehensive review on the Army's policies and practices as to CMTC (Colored). There is one piece of inconclusive evidence that a camp or camps for African Americans might have been conducted by the Third Corps Area sometime in the 1920s. CMTC correspondence Index #19 (National Archives, Suitland Annex) lists the following: "G-1/7547, 2/9/25, M-for TAG drctg. reply be made to letr. from Walter Smith, re CMTC for colored men, in accordance with policy established in CMTC letr. #5, 1/17/23, that writer be advs. to address his application to CT. 3d C.A."

definition, were supporters of the War Department, called attention to the department's dismal record. Stafford King, civilian aide
for Minnesota, in a letter to the War Department dated July 8,
1940, stressed the need for a broader opportunity for African
Americans to serve in national defense.[1]

The War Department's attitude and actions were not so different from that of the rest of American society during the period.
Segregation was institutionalized and, during most of the first half
of the 20th century, overt discrimination against Americans of
African descent wasn't an exclusive practice of the deep South.
Only the famous, such as Joe Louis, the heavyweight champion;
Jesse Owens, the 1936 Olympic record setter; Louis Armstrong,
jazz-music pioneer; Bill ("Bojangles") Robinson, tap dancer and
movie star; or Marian Anderson, great operatic contralto, could
command respect or any serious attention in white America. Even
at that in 1939 the Daughters of the American Revolution banned
Miss Anderson's scheduled concert in Constitution Hall in Washington, D.C. A later outdoor concert in the nation's capital was
arranged by First Lady Eleanor Roosevelt, one of the few influential Americans who displayed the moral courage to publicly
battle bigotry.

In 1924, a year after the War Department denied an African
American's application to CMTC, the NAACP accused the War
Department of having "'Jim Crowed' the Negro. . . . The War
Department is conducting during the summer a large number of
camps for military training. These camps do not simply train
soldiers; they are excellent centers of physical development and
comradeship. To few of these camps, and possibly to none, are
Negroes admitted although the expenses are paid by the United
States government and legally they are open to every American
citizen of the proper age. If, however, enough colored persons
apply, arrangements will be made for special colored camps."[2]

Although there is no clear evidence of any "special colored

camps" being held in the 1920s the subject was, at least, discussed. A Seventh Corps Area report in 1923 stated: "It probably will be necessary to establish one or two small colored camps at places where they can be conducted at small cost for transportation, personnel, and camp preparation. Probably one such camp should be held in Kansas and another in Arkansas or Missouri. It may be practicable to hold these at colored schools where the advantages to the school will be sufficient to pay for use of their facilities."[3] But it appears that no CMTC (Colored) was held in the Seventh Corps Area until 13 years later.

The War Department's foot dragging on the issue of camps for African Americans came to light once more during the 1920s. The April 6, 1927, issue of the *New York Times* was headlined "ARMY BARS NEGRO AT TRAINING CAMP."[4] The article described how George Harris, editor of the *New York News*, a newspaper for African Americans, took up the cause of Marsden V. Burnell of New York City by writing to President Coolidge and protesting the Army's rejection of Burnell's CMTC application. Everett Sanders, Coolidge's secretary, replied, informing Harris that the matter "is being promptly brought to the attention of the officials of the War Department." The *Times* quoted War Department officials as claiming its policy was "to establish a training camp for negroes in each corps area if a minimum of fifty qualified men applied for admission. That number has not qualified in the Second or New York Corps Area [*sic*]." In his letter to the President, Harris quoted from the rejection letter to Burnell signed by Lt. Col. H. W. Fleet, Second Corps Area CMTC Officer. Fleet wrote: "We are not permitted to accept colored men in the C.M.T. Camp in this area. . . . There will be camps for colored young men in Southern States, and of course you are eligible to attend, although it will not be possible to pay your way the entire distance from New York to the camp. I suggest that you send your application to the C.M.T.C. Officer, Fourth Corps Area, Red

Rock Building, Atlanta, Georgia.'"[5] No evidence was found to document that any camps for black candidates were held in Fourth Corps Area.* Another *New York Times* story reported the NAACP having also protested Burnell's exclusion from CMTC. The story quoted Harris saying, "No notice had been given to negro citizens that they might be admitted in units of fifty each to training camps if they presented themselves in such numbers. If the War Department, as reported in the *Times*, has any such plan it has been kept a secret from those most interested. . . . I believe that claim to be mere camouflage.'"[6] The War Department passed the buck back to Headquarters, Second Corps Area for an "investigation." "As you know," Acting Secretary of War Hanford MacNider wrote Harris, "Citizens' Military Training Camps' procurement is de-centralized to corps area commanders."[7] Apparently "Catch 22" was practiced long before Joseph Heller coined the phrase.[8]

The only War Department documents uncovered providing positive proof that CMTC (Colored) training was ever conducted consist of brief reports from the Third, Seventh, and Ninth Corps areas dated 1938 and another from Third Corps Area dated 1939.[9] One report confirms the first camp for African Americans at Fort MacArthur, California, having been scheduled for August 9, 1938. The report shows 85 Basic and 15 Red (Second-year) candidates accepted for Coastal Artillery Corps training. (The 15 Second-year men at Fort MacArthur probably had previous military experience or were members of the Regular Army.) The report carries a note stating: "This is the first colored camp to be held in this [Ninth] Corps Area."

*In May 1938 the Adjutant General responded to a telegram from a reserve officer, 2nd Lt. Frank Edward Smith Jr. of Alexandria, La., who was evidently an African American, not favorably considering his suggestion that a CMTC (Colored) be established that summer in Fourth Corps Area. The reply said that because of the late date (May 9) of Smith's request it was "highly improbable that arrangements can be made for establishing a colored camp in the South during the coming summer." The letter suggested that Smith take the matter up with the Commanding General, Fourth Corps Area. No further information was found.

The other two reports provide evidence that the first Citizens' Military Training Camps (Colored) began in 1936. The first CMTC (Colored) training at Fort Riley, Kansas, and Fort Howard, Maryland, apparently began the summer of 1936 with mostly Basic candidates and a small number of Second-year men.[10] In 1938 Seventh Corps Area reported that 125 candidates had been accepted for the Fort Riley, Kansas, Citizens' Military Training Camp (Colored). Sixty-three African Americans were accepted for the Basic course, 37 for the Red course, 19 for the White course, and 6 Blue candidates were slated to complete the fourth and last year of training. Third Corps Area reported 60 or 90 Basics (depending on the Corps Area's final assigned quota), 75 Reds, 55 Whites, and 20 Blues, for a total of 210 or 240.[11] Once begun the three CMTC (Colored) programs appear to have continued for the remainder of CMTC's existence.

★

Despite the paucity of War Department evidence, there is positive, human proof of the existence of CMTC for African Americans. Lt. Col. Charles M. Bussey, a hero of the Korean War, was one of the charter members of the CMTC (Colored) at Fort MacArthur in 1938, and also attended the next year. Bussey, in the early autobiographical pages of his book *Firefight at Yechon,*[12] told of his CMTC experience. Born and raised in Bakersfield, California, Bussey had attended a racially integrated high school, where he showed an early interest in and aptitude for things military, but was barred from participating in Junior ROTC. The high school's professor of military science did manage to take enough interest in young Bussey to favorably endorse his application for the new camp at Fort MacArthur.[13]

"In due time I was advised officially of my acceptance to a camp that accepted 'colored people.'. . . I left home to go to camp for the first time in 1938, the most exciting and enlightening thirty days of my life.

"This was the finest time of my youth. It was a continuous adventure. . . . I was at camp with other Negro teenagers. That in itself was good for me because I was exposed for the first time to high-quality young black men who had matured in the progressive urban centers of California. These were young men of the highest quality I had ever known."[14] The instruction was provided by a cadre of white officers and black enlisted men from the 25th Infantry Regiment, stationed at Fort Huachuca, Arizona, Bussey said. That first year Bussey took part in a "drill-down" with about 350 other candidates. After several grueling hours of drill, he found himself one of only three remaining on the drill field. Soon it was just Bussey and one other competitor: "'H'at ease.' I relaxed and moved my left foot about ten inches to the left; my competitor simply slumped slightly in place. Either was acceptable by the book but I was thumbed out."[15] Bussey said that being "number two in that environment was a towering success to me." Later he won the camp welterweight boxing trophy and also took the top marksmanship award. Bussey wrote: "When I returned home from CMTC that second year, I was a different, new person—confident, strong, resolute."[16]

★ 23 ★

Out of the Woods, on to Oblivion
1 9 3 6 – 1 9 4 0

Tom, there's going to be a war just as sure as God made little green apples and you're going to be an officer, not a slob enlisted man like your old man," said Thomas Conrow's father in 1937.

In 1936 Hitler's armies had marched undeterred into the Rhineland; Italy's strongman, Mussolini, had directed the invasion and defeat of Ethiopia; and General Franco, with the support of Germany and Italy, was obviously winning the Spanish Civil War. "The American people were taking note of an outside world whose orderly foundations were crumbling as the aggressors of the new German-Italian Axis moved step by threatening step toward domination," wrote Frederick Lewis Allen.[1] It can't be said for certain that the increasingly darker war clouds were the cause, but CMTC applications went up in 1936, with 58,327 young men applying for the program—an increase of 8 percent from 1935. Also, the number of camps was increased by two.

Although New York City undoubtedly had its share of those who, because of various philosophies or causes, were opposed to military preparedness, the nation's largest city wasn't shy about playing the part of cheerleader for patriotism and national defense. For the eighth straight year New York City held an Army Day parade. Described as the "biggest yet" the 1936 parade took two and a half hours to pass Governor Herbert Lehman as he reviewed the 24,000 marchers, including 6,000 CMTC candidates.[2]

Many of the parents of the 31,480 lads who showed up at the 49 camps held in 1936 might have been happy for a four-week respite from their offspring's daily delivery of the latest "knock, knock" joke. (A song from the 1936 movie *Rhythm on the Range* could easily have inspired something similar to this: "Knock, knock." "Who's there?" "Domino." "Domino who?" "Domino Cow Hand!" The airwaves were filled with Bing Crosby singing his latest hit, "I'm an Old Cowhand from the Rio Grande.") On the other hand, the family might have been at least one player short at their Monopoly® board. The new parlor game was one of the nation's hottest sellers despite the Depression or, more likely, because of it. The opportunity to play the part of big-time financier provided vicarious thrills for millions of Americans. Hostesses at CMTC service clubs in 1936 would have been sure to stock several boards and extra Monopoly money for the candidates' use.

Disturbing news from foreign lands couldn't compete with Americans' interest in the presidential election campaign. Franklin D. Roosevelt was nominated for a second term and the Republican party passed over former President Hoover, Senator Vandenberg, and Frank Knox to pick the little-known Alfred Landon, governor of Kansas, as its candidate. Many expected the election to be a close race. The *Literary Digest*, which for years had been conducting election straw votes on a huge scale, predicted a Landon victory. A new pollster, Dr. George Gallup, showed FDR in the lead throughout the campaign, however. Jim Farley, the President's campaign manager, said Roosevelt would carry every state but Maine and Vermont. The incumbent President won by a landslide, carrying every state but those two. The old political saw "as Maine goes, so goes the nation," now more precisely became "as Maine goes, so goes Vermont."[3]

Despite the threatening developments from across the Atlantic, many Americans were more intrigued with the reports from over there of romance between an American woman, Wallis Warfield

Simpson, and Great Britain's sovereign, Edward VIII, what H. L. Mencken called "the greatest news story since the Resurrection."[4] The king's announcement of his abdication on December 11, 1936, was given banner headlines in U.S. newspapers. Having succeeded his father, George V, little more than 10 months before, the love-smitten king would be relegated to the title, Duke of Windsor, and in May 1937 would marry "the woman I love," a divorced American commoner.[5]

Americans began to develop a vague feeling of optimism in 1936, which carried over through the New Year and the inauguration of Roosevelt for a second term. The Secretary of War was also upbeat in his report on the Army's activities of fiscal year 1938. "Popular interest in the citizens [sic] military training camps continues unabated. Neither funds nor facilities have permitted acceptance of the many thousands who have annually applied for enrollment in this popular democratic institution for the instruction of our youths."[6] (This shortage of funds and facilities may have been the War Department's strongest—but unspoken, of course—motivation for failure to promote CMTC applications from African Americans.)

The Secretary of War also reported: "The motor has replaced the horse as the tractive power in the supply trains of practically all our Regular Army and National Guard units. . . . In the procurement of antiaircraft artillery progress has been achieved, as is also true of *mechanized vehicles* [emphasis added]."[7] Progress isn't always immediately recognized by everyone, however. "Our column was marching back to the camp area [Fort Sheridan in the late 1930s], and we heard the damnedest, noisiest racket coming around our column," remembered James Cantwell. "It started loud and it continued to get louder. It sounded much like a bunch of loose metal being mixed in a washing machine. Finally, it had gotten to the head of the column where we were, when what crashed past us was this tank. Remembering it now, it seemed to be about the size of a Volkswagon with this 37-mm or, maybe, even a 20-mm gun sticking out of this strange looking turret. With the size, in relation to the noise it made, it made a perfect end to a very hard day. We roared with laughter to such an extent that I think the driver would have gladly driven over us from one end of the column to the other."

CMTC's figures for 1937—applications, enrollment, number of camps—changed little from the year before.[8] What did change was the nation's fragile economic recovery, which was beginning to unravel by September. Frederick Lewis Allen wrote: "During the latter part of 1936 and the early part of 1937 there had taken place sharp increases in the prices of goods—some of them following increases in wages during the CIO's [the nation's leading labor union] offensive, some of them affected by armament orders from Europe, many of them accentuated by a general impression, among business men, that 'inflation' might be coming and that one had better buy before it was too late."[9*] The nation's Index of Industrial Production, managed by the Federal Reserve Board, stood at 117 in August 1937 and by May 1938 registered a low of 76. The stock market dropped steadily from September 1937 to March 1938, racking up lows not seen since the collapse of 1929–1932. In the space of a few months two million men lost their jobs. On January 1, 1938, the government announced the results of its first national unemployment census, showing that at least 7.8 million Americans were jobless and saying that unemployment might actually total more than 10 million.

These distressing developments may have contributed to

---

*A look at some of the prices in New York City during the second half of 1937 makes it difficult for today's reader to imagine them as inflated. A $127 sofa on sale for $69.50; Eastern Steamship line offering a round trip to Boston from New York for $8.50; the *New York Times* daily issue still costing two cents, although it would go up to three cents the next year; "Made to Measure" men's top coats on sale for $33.50; and men's shoes $6 to $7 a pair, with "bench-made grade" selling for $8.50. (*NYT* ads appearing between July–December 1937.)

Roosevelt's proposing in his fiscal year 1939 budget, which his Administration had pledged would be a balanced one,[10] to cut CMTC's appropriation to $1 million from the nearly $2.3 million authorized the previous year. The popularity of CMTC with Congress once more paid off, and the full amount was restored to the Army appropriations bill.[11] Perhaps reflecting the recession, almost 8,000 more men applied for camp in 1938 than had the year before. Fifty camps were conducted, and about 4,500 more men completed the four-week course than did in 1937.

In 1938 the radio was a convenient way to temporarily escape the tough times. If with maturity comes controversy then commercial radio was definitely maturing. Early in 1938 the Federal Communications Commission (FCC) reprimanded the National Broadcasting Company for airing what the commission considered to have been a lewd program. Mae West, Don Ameche, and Charlie McCarthy, Edgar Bergen's popular dummy, performed a skit titled "Adam and Eve." The FCC said the network should have curbed material "offensive to the great mass of right-thinking, clean-minded American citizens."[12] Radio fans who on Sunday night, October 30, were tuned to NBC-Blue network's "Chase and Sanborn Hour," starring Bergen and Charlie, missed the scariest, most controversial program ever broadcast on American radio. Twenty-three-year-old Orson Welles, producer and one of the principal actors of the "Mercury Theatre on the Air" series on CBS, dramatized H. G. Wells's *The War of the Worlds,* and did such a realistic job that thousands of gullible Americans believed Martians had landed in New Jersey.[13] Perhaps the events of a month earlier had contributed to the irrational cases of nerves the program revealed. On September 29 in Munich, Germany, British Prime Minister Neville Chamberlain and Premier Edouard Daladier of France signed a pact with Hitler and Mussolini, agreeing to Germany's annexation of the Sudeten region of Czechoslovakia—an act of appeasement labeled by Chamberlain as "peace in our time."

★

The camps Bill Bentson attended in 1937 and 1938 took on special meaning for him because of the post commander: "Brig. Gen. George C. Marshall, Jr. was commanding Vancouver Barracks the first two years I was at CMTC, in 1937 and '38. I was fortunate one year to be one of the cadets invited to his quarters socially. We were asked by the general how we liked the camp, etc. He was most hospitable and congenial to us cadets. Our main attention fell on his stepdaughter Molly. She was the center of attraction during our visit. We would often go out of our way to walk by the quarters and wave to Molly, if she was on the front veranda or the back stoop. On one occasion four of us serenaded at the rear of the quarters, with a few barbershop quartet songs, primarily for the benefit of Molly."

Marshall's experience with the summer training of young volunteers went back to the program's concept. As a captain in 1916 he was cadre for the West Coast's version of Plattsburg's "Tired Businessmen's Camp" conducted at the plush grounds of the Del Monte Hotel in Monterey, California. According to Marshall's boss, Gen. J. Franklin Bell, headquartered at the Presidio of San Francisco, the volunteer trainees were "all the hot bloods of San Francisco. I saw more Rolls-Royces and other fine cars around there than I have ever seen collected." It was Captain Marshall's job to whip them into shape, which he did with a firm effectiveness that earned him the respect of the "hot bloods" and won him the nickname "Dynamite."[14]

In 1923, as a lieutenant colonel, Marshall again was closely associated with CMTC when he accompanied General Pershing on a nationwide tour of the camps.[15] When he took command of Vancouver Barracks, Marshall demonstrated a special empathy for the program. The 1937 CMTC after-action report from Vancouver Barracks bears the mark of having been drafted, at least in part, by Marshall himself. Replete with sound, logical recommendations for changes in CMTC, his letter addressed "the

George C. Marshall wore the eagles of a full colonel when he posed for this photo in 1919. With demobilization after World War I, Marshal would revert to his permanent rank of major, but by 1923 had advanced to lieutenant colonel. (National Archives.)

wholesale fabrication of ages" (a situation as old as the program itself), and recommended lowering the age to 16 "for boys well advanced physically who have finished high school or entered college." It also urged the War Department to "procure a decent uniform, suitable to very young men and which will serve to advertise the CMTC more favorably." The final recommendation was to adopt the "new drill regulations proposed several years ago" thus overcoming "the undue wastage of time in training CMTC boys in our archaic regulations."[16] The ideas of great men so often read simply as good common sense.

★

As 1939 began, funding for CMTC again seemed in jeopardy. The President's fiscal year 1940 budget proposed to cut $307,700 from CMTC.[17] Once more Congress came to the program's rescue and the usual $2 million-plus was restored. Except for conducting one less camp, with a concomitant drop in attendance of about 1,300, the 1939 operation of CMTC was little changed from the year before.[18]

The U.S. economy's recovery, slow as it was, had stalled. Then early in 1939 came a diversion from the daily gloom on a far grander scale than the escape provided by either radio or the movies. "On the morning of Sunday, April 30, 1939, the gates of the New York World's Fair were thrown open. The theme of the Fair was 'The World of Tomorrow'; the opening ceremonies were held in a vast enclosure called the 'Court of Peace.' Could anybody in that throng of thousands, gathered under a blue sky in which hung mountainous clouds, fail to reflect upon the question ironically posed by those two phrases?" pondered social historian Frederick Lewis Allen.[19] Two months earlier the Golden Gate Exposition in San Francisco opened, providing the people on the West Coast also with a taste of how much better the currently miserable world could be through the advances of science.

During the two years the New York World's Fair operated, CMTC was given special attention. Wednesday, August 2, 1939, was declared "Citizens' Military Training Camps Day." At the Court of Peace the CMTC battalion from Fort Hancock, New Jersey, gave a drill demonstration and Fort Hancock's 52nd Coastal Artillery Band played a concert for the audience of 5,000. "While the C.M.T.C. battalion . . . was the only participating unit, the audience included several hundred former CMTC students and many who had earned reserve officer commissions through training," the *New York Times* reported in its lead paragraph.[20] Two Fort Hancock CMTC alumni, Donald Martin and Fred Renken, remembered the day. "Our boat [from Sandy Hook, New Jersey] docked right at the fairgrounds," Martin recalled. "We felt very proud to be able to parade for all the visitors from around the world."

CMTC Day at the fair was repeated the next year, with 225 candidates from Fort Hancock participating. Although the candidates at Fort Dix weren't lucky enough to get a free trip to the World's Fair, the 2,000-man CMTC regiment passed in review for the visiting commissioner general of the fair's British Pavilion, C. M. Pickthall, when he visited their camp.[21]

On their way home from CMTC training in Monterey, Tom

Conrow and a buddy took a detour to visit San Francisco's version of what the future promised. The Golden Gate Exposition was situated on man-made Treasure Island, which was built in San Francisco Bay to serve as grounds for the fair. The fair had gained most of its nationwide fame from reports of the "scandalous" terpsichore of fan-dancer Sally Rand. Conrow remembered seeing one young woman billed as "Miss America," who he said was "bare as a radish," and Sally Rand, who was "not very bare." He said they also took in "lots of wondrous sights for a couple of country boys."

In the two years that the fairs on both U.S. coasts were entertaining the public and amazing them with promises of the future, Europe had become a battleground, as Hitler invaded first Poland, and then Norway and France, with the British Isles his obvious next target. Americans also had to face the sad truth that the Depression persisted. A news story datelined Fort Hancock, New Jersey, May 22, 1939, reported a fatal accident in which CMTC was indirectly involved. Walter Connelly, a WPA worker, was killed and four others injured in the collapse of a concrete building that was to have housed a CMTC headquarters. Connelly, 44, who left a wife and five children, was crushed by the falling roof. The four who were hurt had been shingling the roof with Connelly. The paragraph providing details of Connelly's background starkly illustrated the realities of the nation's economic problems: "Mr. Connelly formerly was a customer's man for the New York brokerage firm of Post & Flagg and was connected with its Newark branch. He was a graduate of Columbia University and before joining the brokerage firm had devoted himself to chemistry."[22]

John Yount, who signed up for CMTC in 1940, remembered the tough times: "I was 19 at the time and jumped at the chance to go. The Great Depression was still on and jobs for teens were few and far between."

★

With Congress passing a multi-billion dollar defense appropriations bill for fiscal year 1941, CMTC's annual $2,275,000 was approved without a hitch. The 1940 camps numbered 49 and about 1,500 more men completed the training than in 1939. For the first time since 1931 orders were issued to more than 40,000 men.[23]

Julius Ochs Adler and Theodore Roosevelt, Jr., as well as many other living alumni of the Plattsburg Movement, saw history repeat itself in 1940 when Army corps area commanders were authorized to establish what the War Department called a "special course for business and professional men, Citizens' Military Training Camps."[24] A week after the announcement of the revived "Tired Business Men's Camps," President Roosevelt appointed Henry Stimson, a Republican, as Secretary of War. Stimson had served as Secretary of War in William Howard Taft's administration and had given early encouragement and support to General Leonard Wood's efforts that spawned the Plattsburg Movement.[25]

Ten special businessmen's camps for volunteers from age 25 to 50 were conducted that summer; one camp in each corps area except the Eighth where two were held. Each training site was co-located with a regular CMTC, where the volunteers, who paid their own expenses, received the four-week Basic course.[26] Among the 2,200 reporting were some of the Eastern "patrician" class, the best known of whom was Winthrop Rockefeller.[27] Although members of reserve components, such as the National Guard and the Organized Reserve Corps, weren't eligible for the special camps, the new emphasis on military readiness provided more opportunities for reservists to perform periods of active duty. Among reservists with prominent names, none could claim more distinction than the reserve captain commanding a reconnaissance unit at Fort Knox. The two-week tour of Senator Henry Cabot Lodge, Jr. of Massachusetts was reported by the Associated Press.[28] "The captain supervises the tricky business of manoeuvering [*sic*] cars across ditches, through underbrush and whatever conditions the countryside presents."

As the Army corps areas and the MTCA were busy recruiting for the 20th CMTC and the special businessmen's camps, military mobilization and the nation's first peacetime draft were on the immediate horizon.[29] It didn't take a crystal ball to predict the future of CMTC—the program didn't have one. Its faithful voice, the *New York Times,* closed 20 years of CMTC coverage with a modest story on page 17:

"Washington, D.C., Sept. 27: Citizens' Military Training Camps will be suspended during the summer of 1941, the War Department stated today. . . ."[30]

Official notice came in the fiscal year 1941 *Report of the Secretary of the War*: "In order to concentrate all available means and facilities on the vitally important and immediate task of training the combatant forces, C.M.T. Camps have been suspended for the fiscal year 1942."[31] A post script—almost an afterthought, with a touch of irony—appeared two years later:

AR 350-2200
C 1

MILITARY EDUCATION

CITIZENS' MILITARY TRAINING CAMPS

CHANGES   WAR DEPARTMENT,
NO. 1   Washington 25, D.C., 29 June 1943

AR 350-2200, 15 December 1938, is suspended for the duration of the war.

[A.G. 354.1 (18 Jun 43).] (C1, 29 Jun 43.)

BY ORDER OF THE SECRETARY OF WAR:

G. C. MARSHALL
Chief of Staff

OFFICIAL:
J. A. ULIO,
Major General,
   The Adjutant General.

DISTRIBUTION:
  B.

What It Was,
What It Wasn't

1 9 2 1 — 1 9 4 0

As popular and well publicized as CMTC appears to have been during its 20-year life, it still suffered a degree of obscurity and longed for a clearer identity.

Even though Maj. Gen. Gray and Gen. Conway had been West Point classmates and later served together, it wasn't until 60 years later, as contributors to this book, that they discovered they both had been CMTC candidates. "I was surprised that Ted was an ex-CMTCer," Gray said. "We never discussed that in all the time we spent together at [Fort] Benning, West Point, Washington, and Korea. I recall when we were both platoon leaders in A Co., 29th Infantry at Benning, he often mentioned his service as a soldier at the Presidio of San Francisco, but we never delved any further than that into our younger days." Gray also said he was surprised to learn of CMTC's continuation through the austere 1930s, having never been made aware of its existence during his pre-World War II service.

CMTC's identity problem seems to have been an inherent one. Congress in 1920 had authorized the Secretary of War to maintain schools or camps for military instruction, "with a view to their appointment as reserve officers or noncommissioned officers, of such warrant officers, enlisted men, and civilians as may be selected upon their own applications."[1] Later President Coolidge, the second Commander in Chief to have CMTC under his "command," declared the camps to be "essentially schools in citizenship."[2]

A sampling of some the statements in the Secretary of War's annual reports also reveals the lack of a clear-cut definition of the program's objectives: "[1924] The future of the C.M.T.C. is a matter of much interest. On the one hand, it may be regarded as an activity entirely separate from our military system, provided for the purpose of giving physical and military training to large numbers of young men. On the other hand it may be regarded as a definite feeder for the National Guard and the Organized Reserves."[3]

"[1930] Few attend a sufficient number of years to complete the curriculum and qualify themselves for commission in the Officers' Reserve Corps. The chief benefit to the country flowing from the citizens' military training camps lies in improved citizenship qualifications which can not fail to result from their influence. It is apparent that the camps do not directly serve to promote any military objective. The chief benefit to the Army lies in the increased confidence in its personnel on the part of the civilian population which has followed from the many contacts incident to the conduct of the camps."[4]

"[1934] The *citizens' military training camps* [italics in original] are also feeders for the Officers' Reserve Corps, but are principally necessary as a source of supply of partially trained individuals for building up additional military formations in emergency. Their value is unquestioned, and the camps should provide 1 month's training for not less than 50,000 young men annually."[5]

"[1935] Citizens' Military Training Camps [the War Department never settled on upper or lower case when referring to the program] were established to afford military training to those volunteers among American youth who were denied the privilege of attending college. . . . A graduate of the complete course becomes eligible for a commission in the Officers' Reserve Corps.

However, this training is not lost upon those who do not pursue it to the end, since their value as prospective noncommissioned officers in a mobilization is greatly increased."[6]

If the paragraph above wasn't drafted by the Army's Chief of Staff at the time, General Douglas MacArthur, at least it expressed an opinion he had previously stated. In defending CMTC funding before Congress in 1935 MacArthur described CMTC as the only program permitting sons of the poor to prepare for service.[7]

President Hoover, in a message provided to the Military Training Camps Association (MTCA), endorsed the idea of CMTC, but did little to clarify its purpose: "The citizens' military training camps have through ten years proved themselves important agencies of physical and moral health in the individual and of civic welfare in the nation.

"The willingness of young men to devote a month to this training program for better citizenship is proof of 'goodwill' in the generation on which will presently devolve the maintenance of our social and political institutions.

"I commend the citizens' military training camps to all fathers and mothers and to young men of suitable age in the hope and belief that the camps will show themselves as useful in the future as they have been in the past."[8]

In the early 1930s other elected officials also were making statements about CMTC—and not all of them favorable. One of the most outspoken critics of the program was Representative Ross Collins of Mississippi (naturally a Democrat in those days) and chairman of the House appropriations subcommittee. The Mississippi congressman was described by some opponents, including the *Jackson Mississippi News*, as a pacifist,[9] and more gently by the *New York Times* as a "sometimes misguided friend of economy."[10] Early in 1931 Collins had attacked compulsory military education in the schools as an "un-American peacetime conscription of boys, which is increasingly arousing civic and religious bodies to protest. We find that they are teaching the boys [in CMTC

One of the officers who was "present at the creation," Douglas MacArthur accompanied Maj. Gen. W. A. Mann at Camp Mills on Long Island, New York, in 1918. As a captain before World War I he assisted Army Chief of Staff Leonard Wood in establishing the Plattsburg Movement. In the mid-1920s as a young major general and a corps area commander he actively promoted CMTC. As Army Chief of Staff in the early 1930s he battled Congress to save annual appropriations for the program. (National Archives.)

and ROTC] to 'serve their country' by offering them prettified social activities instead of honest military preparedness."[11]

In 1933 when CMTC funding was under even greater scrutiny and was almost completely eliminated, Representative Collins' ally on the subcommittee, Representative Thomas L. Blanton of Texas, was quoted as characterizing the young men attending CMTC as "ring-around-the rosy boys."[12] The *New York Times*

attributed the remark to Collins, helping him maintain his reputation as the chief CMTC naysayer.[13]

American mothers were quoted, perhaps apocryphally in a case
or two, during the subcommittee debate. Congressman Henry
Barbour of California, in speaking for CMTC, said many war
mothers had visited him to say they felt that their sons who were
killed in France might be "alive today if they had been properly
trained." According to the *Times* Collins, however, had the last
word: "Mr. Collins ended the argument against the camps. He
suggested that if such a reserve were to be maintained it should
be turned over to the National Guard.

"'But no, that wouldn't do,' he [Collins] said. 'I know of a
mother who said she would not send her boy to the NG [National
Guard] camps because they do not rate as high socially as the
Citizens' Military Training Camps.'"[14] So much for MacArthur's
portrayal of CMTC as a plebeian program.

Representative Collins was correct in saying that CMTC had
other detractors, although there is little evidence to support his
contention that "civic bodies"—at least those of the main-
stream—were among those protesting military training. It is true,
however, that at least part of the Presbyterian Church[15] and later
the entire Methodist Episcopal Church[16] expressed misgivings
about mandatory military training in schools.* But in each case
CMTC was given at least lukewarm support. Nonetheless, in

---

*At the 1926 convention of the General Assembly of the New York Presbytery
a resolution condemning universal military training was voted down. The *New
York Times* story (June 1, 1926, pp. 1, 11) went on to state that a resolution
commending CMTC was passed. In a letter to the editor (June 2, p. 24) the writer
claimed the CMTC resolution was tabled rather than passed. In another *Times*
story (May 22, 1928, p. 28) the Methodist Episcopal Church's Quadrennial General
Conference condemned mandatory college ROTC. One of the church's officials
explained that there "was no opposition to military training camps or for effective
military training in colleges and universities [voluntary, apparently]. Strong opposition to any kind of military training in high schools was voiced, however."

retired Maj. Gen. William Weigel's view there were enough ministers who opposed military camps and preparedness to prompt him to tell a Rotary Club audience that such clergymen should "stick to their knitting and keep out of politics."[17]

Summer military training for American youths was considered important—and ominous—enough to earn condemnation by at least two of the nation's scholar-pacifists. Oswald Garrison Villard, who probably would have preferred the title "military defense critic" to the emotionally charged label "pacifist," wrote: "From the very beginning of the Citizens' Military Training Camp movement there was a twofold objective: instruction in the rudiments of military drill and the inculcation of military and nationalistic doctrines."[18] In support of this belief he quoted Walter Millis, a fellow scholar who seemed to march to the same drummer as Villard: "And as early as 1913 he [General Wood] had evolved the most subtle of all engines with which he was finally to convert the United States to militarism." Millis went on to briefly describe the "Plattsburg Idea," and concluded the paragraph with: "The camps . . . were designed from the start to be (as their successors still are today) not practical schools of war but seminaries whence propagandists for preparedness might be distributed through the civil population."[19]

It is doubtful if many Plattsburg alumni would have objected to being called "propagandists for preparedness." That is exactly what motivated them to form the MTCA. The MTCA's role in the 20 years of CMTC has been frequently mentioned in this account, and if any point has been made, it is the association's importance in promoting and supporting CMTC. Yet the MTCA had its flaws, inconsistencies, and inefficiencies, just as does any organization, particularly a volunteer one. The chief chronicler of the MTCA, John Garry Clifford, in his excellent history of the Plattsburg Movement, had this to say of the MTCA after World War I: "To facilitate recruitment for the CMTC, the national headquarters of the MTCA moved from New York to Chicago in the winter of 1922–1923, and Charles B. Pike, a wealthy and ambitious Chicagoan, was elected chairman of the Executive Committee. Thereafter the influence and interest of the original Plattsburgers diminished considerably. . . . Because Pike agreed with the army's emphasis on citizenship training in the CMTC, the policy of the association came to reflect his views—much to the chagrin of those who still clung to the banner of universal military training. . . . By the mid-1930s, therefore, the MTCA had evolved to the point where all decisions were made in Chicago, and these decisions usually reflected the isolationist mood of Middle America."[20]*

In a 1923 letter to the Army's Adjutant General, the commander of the Sixth Corps Area, also headquartered in Chicago, discussed the utilization of the MTCA in recruiting for CMTC. While attempting to be as diplomatic as possible it was apparent that he felt the association should take a secondary role to the Army, both active and reserve, in CMTC recruiting. He wrote: "The opinion is held by some officers that with our comparatively large group of Reserve Officers we are in close enough contact with the civil population, and that an organization such as the Military Training Camps Association has no cause for further

---

*Although the MTCA, operating out of an office on East Hyde Park Blvd. in Chicago, ultimately faded away in the 1950s, one of its legacies remains. In 1922 Secretary of War John W. Weeks formally recognized the association as "a civilian agency cooperating with the War Department in fostering the voluntary military training of civilians." The secretary authorized the appointment of aides to the Secretary of War. (Undated, unsigned brief paper on the history of CMTC, p. 4.) This concept survives today, with one or more volunteer Civilian Aides to the Secretary of the Army appointed in each state and one each representing the Army areas within the U.S. (War Dept. directive dated November 22, 1922, and undated, unsigned "History of the Secretary of the Army's Civilian Aide Program.") Perhaps the zenith of the association's political clout came with the passage of the Selective Service Act of 1940. (Clifford and Spencer, *The First Peacetime Draft*, University Press of Kansas, 1986.)

existence. I do not agree with this opinion. I believe that the assistance of the [MTCA] . . . is most valuable and should be welcomed even though that assistance amounted only to the approval of our plan and the public announcement of such approval."[21]

Considering that many of the MTCA's original members later became ranking officers in the Officers' Reserve Corps—Col. Julius Ochs Adler for instance—the association had a puzzling reaction to the War Department's decision in 1928 to use some Organized Reserve units to assist with CMTC training. The units did well in 1928, so the next year the Secretary of War directed that reserve units would be used in at least one camp in each of the nine corps areas.[22] The authors of *Twice the Citizen*, a history of the Army Reserve, described the public reaction as immediate—and unfavorable. "The Hearst newspapers editorialized against the use of Organized Reserve units at the Camps. . . . On February 18, 1929, Charles B. Pike, Chief Civilian Aide to War Secretary Davis, forwarded copies of letters protesting the use of Organized Reserve Officers in the CMTC. The underlying reason for the protest against the Reserve officers probably was less with doubts of their effectiveness than with a perception that the prestige of the CMTC was diminished by not having a cadre of Regular Army personnel only."[23]

The protests went for naught, however, and Organized Reserve officers and units continued through the remainder of CMTC to provide a sizeable and relatively effective cadre for the program. According to *Twice the Citizen* this was the greatest contribution of CMTC. "Considering the small number of men who received their commissions through the Camps, the only way to justify Army expenditures on the CMTC is that the men of the ORC received valuable leadership experience."[24] It's unknown whether the writers were aware that the per capita cost of CMTC training never exceeded the high of $69 reached in 1925, and had fallen to $61 in 1940. The "hidden costs," i.e., pay and allowances of Regular Army personnel detailed to the training, was estimated at $50,000 in 1925.[25]

To argue the CMTC case, pro or con, in dollars and cents is pointless. Most purely objective evaluations of the program, based on hard dollars and statistics, would not rate the program's 20 years any higher than did the authors of *Twice the Citizen*. When presented with the favorable memories and strong endorsements of hundreds of men who were there, it is difficult not to join them in believing CMTC was something special. In several cases CMTC alumni went so far as to say that CMTC training saved their lives during World War II. A far more frequent and modest reaction was that CMTC training, even if only one year, made the transition into wartime training much more comfortable. Those who have served in the military know how valuable it is to be able from the start to do simple drill moves and fold a hospital corner on a barracks bunk.

Whatever problems CMTC had with its identity, the fact that it never reached President Harding's 100,000-men-a-year goal, or that it wasn't a prolific source of new lieutenants—these things mattered not at all to our group of alumni. Obviously the CMTC experience enriched their young lives and continues to occupy a special place in their hearts and minds.[26] In fact, those who contributed to this account may consider its title to be a misnomer. To them those summers have never been forgotten.

At least 50 of this book's contributors said they believed a program similar to CMTC was needed today—several acknowledging that modern-day camps would have to be sexually integrated. Could a program similar to CMTC be successful today? It is doubtful the program our CMTC alumni knew could be reestablished now, more than 50 years later. The fact must be faced—believing CMTC would fit in today's America is an exercise in nostalgia.

In 1981 the subject of Citizens' Military Training Camps arose briefly from its grave when the House Armed Services Committee directed the Department of Defense (DOD) to study the old volunteer training plan as a way to beef up the All-Volunteer Force.[27] If the study ever made it from one Pentagon "in" basket to another DOD "out" basket, it was never publicly revealed. The Clinton administration's national service program for young Americans is now law, but it is a far different concept than was CMTC—operating in what is now a far different nation.

Although now a relic of the past, during its 20-year existence Citizens' Military Training Camps surely made a positive contribution to America.

★ ★ ★

Names of CMTC Alumni Quoted*

Name, Current Hometown, Birthplace	CMTC Data
Bruce Armstrong Carmichael, Calif. Birthplace not provided	Mid- to late-1930s Ft. Dix, N.J.
Col. Donald Armstrong Ft. Monmouth, N.J. Born Roselle Park, N.J.	1923–1924 Plattsburg Brks., N.Y. 1924–1926 Madison Brks., N.Y.
Maj. William ("Bill") Bentson Brisbane, Queensland, Australia Born Silverton, Ore.	1937–1939 Vancouver Brks., Wash.
Lt. Col. Willis Bliss Manhattan Beach, Calif. Born Hollywood, Calif.	1934–1936 Presidio of Monterey, Calif.
Col. Clyde Boden Arlington, Va. Born Shamokin, Pa.	1938 Ft. Hoyle, Md.
Alexander Borysewich Roseville, Mich. Born New York, N.Y.	1936 Ft. Dix, N.J.
Lt. Col. Harold Bourgoin, USAF Bellevue, Wash. Born St. Louis, Mo.	1940 Jefferson Brks., Mo.
Lt. Col. Joseph Brennan, USAF Upland, Calif. Birthplace not provided	1938–1939 Ft. Meade, Md.

*Those who are listed with a military rank are retired and were in the U.S. Army unless another branch of service is listed.

Gerold Breuer
El Paso, Tex.
Born Cleveland, Ohio

1928–1929 Ft. Benjamin Harrison, Ind.

William Buning
Orlando, Fla.
Born Dayton, Ohio

1936–1939 Ft. Screven, Ga.,
Commissioned through CMTC

James Cantwell
Chicago, Ill.
Born Depue, Ill.

1936–1938, Ft. Sheridan, Ill.

Lt. Col. Chester Carpenter, CPA
Cantonsville, MD
Birthplace not provided

1937 Plattsburg Brks., N.Y.
1938–1939 Ft. Hancock, N.J.

Lt. Cmdr. Eugene Chase, USNR
Pensacola, Fla.
Born Britt, Iowa

1930–1931 Ft. Crook, Neb.

Lt. Col. Thomas Conrow, USAF
Spokane, Wash.
Born Pasadena, Calif.

1938–1939 Presidio of Monterey, Calif.
1940 Ft. Ord, Calif.

Gen. Theodore Conway
St. Petersburg, Fla.
Born Vallejo, Calif.

1924–1927 Del Monte, Monterey, Calif.

Richard Corbyn
Amarillo, Tex.
Birthplace not provided

1930 Jefferson Brks., Mo.
1932 Camp Bullis, Tex.
1933 Camp Pike, Ark.
Commissioned through CMTC, CMTC
officer in 1935, 1938, 1939 at Camp Bullis

Lt. Col. Leland Cubbage
Austin, Tex.
Birthplace not provided

1932 Ft. Sheridan, Ill.
1933 Jefferson Brks., Mo.
1934–1935 Ft. Sheridan, Ill.

Lt. Col. Ray Dearth
Okeechobee, Fla.
Born Frankfort, Ind.

1931–1933 and 1938
Ft. Benjamin Harrison, Ind.
Commissioned through CMTC

Lt. Col. Lawrence Doherty
Drexel Hill, Pa.
Born Philadelphia, Pa.

1929–1930 Ft. Eustis, Va.
1931 Ft. Meade, Md.

Maj. Arthur Dorie
Cocoa Beach, Fla.
Born, New York, N.Y.

1940 Ft. Dix, N.J

Col. James Duncan, USAF
Alameda, Calif.
Born Germantown, Ill.

1940 Jefferson Brks., Mo.

Mark Eastin
Madisonville, Ky.
Born Sturgis, Ky.

1921–1924 Camp Knox, Ky.

M. Sgt. Russell Eberhardt
Granite Falls, Minn.
Born Paris, Ark.

1931 Ft. Leavenworth, Kans.
1932 Camp Pike, Ark.

Capt. Jack Ellwood
Portland, Ore.
Born Coquille, Ore.

1938 Vancouver Barracks, Wash.

Lt. Col. Fred Featherstone
Port Charlotte, Fla.
Born Arlington, Ky.

1935–1938 Ft. Screven, Ga.
Commissioned through CMTC

Lt. Col. Robert Fox, PhD, USAF
Deland, Fla.
Born Cleveland, Ohio

1935–1938 Ft. Benjamin Harrison, Ind.
Commissioned through CMTC

Brig. Gen. Alfred Freedman,
N.Y. Guard
Franklin Square, N.Y.
Birthplace not provided

1932–1933 Ft. Dix, N.J.
1934–1935 Madison Brks., N.Y.

CWO Elmer Froewiss, USN
Bremerton, Wash.
Born Brooklyn, N.Y.

1937 Ft. Dix, N.J.

John Gordon
Middleburgh, N.Y.
Born Brooklyn, N.Y.

1940 Ft. Dix, N.J.

Maj. Hugh Graham
Winfield, Kans.
Born Winfield, Kans.

1940 Ft. Riley, Kans.

Maj. Gen. David Gray
Golden Beach, Fla.
Born Evansville, Ind.

1927 Camp Knox, Ky.

Col. Frank Gregory
Del Rey Oaks, Calif.
Born Minneapolis, Minn.

1928, 1932, 1933 Ft. MacArthur, Calif.
Commissioned through CMTC
CMTC officer at Ft. MacArthur 1936

Lt. Cmdr. Russell Haag, USN
Palo Alto, Calif.
Born Eden Valley, Minn.

1935–1936 Presidio of Monterey, Calif.

Herman ("Pat") Herst
Boca Raton, Fla.
Born New York, N.Y.

1927–1930, Vancouver Brks., Wash.

Col. Ralph Hofmann   1937 Ft. Meade, Md.
Columbia, S.C.
Born Ft. Mills, Philippines

Daniel Hughes   1932–1933 Ft. Brady, Mich.
Seven Springs, Fla.
Born Perth, Ontario, Canada

Chap.(Col.) William Huntley   1935 Ft. Snelling, Minn.
Elk River, Minn.
Born Morris, Minn.

CWO Paul Keough, USN   1937–1938 Ft. Devens, Mass.
Columbia, Md.   1939–1940 Ft. Ethan Allen, Vt.
Born Cambridge, Mass.

William Knolle   1940 Plattsburg Brks., N.Y.
Richland, Wash.
Born Monroe, N.Y.

Maj. Frank H. Kreger   1934 Ft. Thomas, Ky.
Cincinnati, Ohio
Born Cincinnati, Ohio

Col. Jean Lambert, USAF   1931–1934 Ft. Snelling, Minn.
Annandale, Va.   Commissioned through CMTC
Born Mankata, Minn.   CMTC officer, Ft. Snelling 1936

Col. Paul LaPierre   1935 Ft. Devens, Mass.
Port Charlotte, Fla.   1936–1938 Ft. Ethan Allen, Vt.
Born Leominster, Mass.

C. A. ("Mac") McCaffrey   1940 Ft. Dix, N.Y.
Ft. Collins, Colo.
Born Newark, N.J.

F. B. McNutt, D.O.   1922 Ft. Meade, Md.
Salem, W.Va.   1923–1924 Ft. Monroe, Va.
Born Claysville, Pa.

Cmdr. Donald Martin, USNR   1937 Ft. Dix, N.J.
Pomona, Calif.   1938 Ft. Hancock, N.J.
Born Mineola, N.Y.

Richard Matteson, D.V.M.   1940 Camp Custer, Mich.
Brookston, Ind.
Born Hamilton, Ohio

Lt. Col. Norris Maxwell   1937–1939 Ft. Bliss, Tex.
San Angelo, Tex.
Born El Paso, Tex.

Col. Lawrence Mayland, USAF
Austin, Tex.
Born Los Angeles, Calif.

1938 Madison Brks., N.Y.
1939–1940 Pine Camp, N.Y.
Commissioned through CMTC

Col. Wilfred Menegus
Escondido, Calif.
Born Passaic, N.J.

1924 Plattsburg Brks., N.Y.

Lt. Col. John Middlebrooks
Kailua, Hawaii.
Born Camphill, Ala.

1934 Ft. Barrancas, Fla.

Lt. Col. Stanley Milkowski
Springfield, Pa.
Born Chrome (now Carteret), N.Y.

1931, 1934–1936 Ft. Hancock, N.J.
Commissioned through CMTC

lst Lt. Robert Miller
San Pedro, Calif.
Born Minneapolis, Minn.

1937–1939 Presidio of Monterey, Calif.
Commissioned through CMTC

Samuel Miller, M.D.
San Francisco, Calif
Born New York, N.Y.

1925 Ft. Custer, Mich.

Lt. Col. John Moale
Melbourne, Fla.
Born San Francisco, Calif.

1937 Presidio of San Francisco, Calif.
1938 Presidio of Monterey, Calif.

William Russell Moher
Nashua, N.H.
Birthplace not provided

1932 Ft. McKinley, Maine,
1934–1936 Ft. Ethan Allen, Vt.

Col. Fred Moore
Novato, Calif.
Born Toledo, Ohio

1939–1940 Ft. Benjamin Harrison, Ind.

Col. James Munday, USAF
Savannah, Ga.
Birthplace not provided

1931 Jefferson Brks., Mo.
1932–1934 Ft. Sheridan, Ill.

George Myers
Dallas, Tex.
Born Denton, Tex.

1940 Camp Bullis, Tex.

Col. Roscoe Norman, USAF
Bradenton, Fla.
Born Kokomo, Ind.

1934–1937 Ft. Benjamin Harrison, Ind.
Commissioned through CMTC

Dr. William Ommert, D.V.M.
Temecula, Calif.
Born Oakland, Calif.

1932–1935 Presidio of Monterey, Calif.

Rear Adm. Richard ("Red") Patterson, 1921 Plattsburg Brks., N.Y.
USNR
Dobbs Ferry, N.Y.
Birthplace not provided

Russell Price   1939 Ft. Hoyle, Md. and Ft. Meade, Md.
Wilmington, Del.
Birthplace not provided

Capt. John Pritchard   1937–1939 Ft. Benjamin Harrison, Ind.
Phoenix, Ariz.
Born Manila, Philippines

Lt. Col. Estes Proffer   1928 Jefferson Brks., Mo.
Thousand Oaks, Calif.
Born Cotton Plant, Ark.

Edward Randall   1929–1932 Ft. Brady, Mich.
Essexville, Mich.   Commissioned through CMTC
Birthplace not provided

Lt. Col. John ("Jack") Reeside   1936–1939 Ft. Meade, Md.
Fayetteville, N.C.   Commissioned through CMTC
Born Washington, D.C.

Lt. Col. Fred Renken, USAF   1936–1939 Ft. Hancock, N.J.
Telford, Pa.
Born Long Island, N.Y.

Col. Howard ("Dusty") Rhodes   1940 Plattsburg Brks., N.Y.
Colorado Springs, Colo.
Born Los Angeles, Calif.

Lt. Col. Darrel Rippeteau   1934 Ft. Crook, Neb.
Delray Beach, Fla. (winter)   1935–1937 Ft. Snelling, Minn.
Alexandria Bay, N.Y. (summer)   Commissioned through CMTC
Born Clay Center, Neb.

Col. Cecil E. Roberts   1935–1938 Ft. Sill, Okla.
Ft. Worth, Tex.   Commissioned through CMTC
Born Burkburnett, Tex.

Bruce Romick   1939 Ft. Des Moines, Iowa
Oklahoma City, Okla.
Born Traer, Iowa

Abe ("Bud") Rubel   1937–1938 Ft. McClellan, Ala.
Memphis, Tenn.
Born Corinth, Miss.

Lt. Col. Chandler Rudicel Hutchinson, Kans. Born Rush Center, Kans.	1923–1925 Ft. Leavenworth, Kans. 1926 Ft. Snelling, Minn. 1927 Ft. Leavenworth, Kans. Commissioned through CMTC CMTC officer, 1935, 1940 Ft. Leaven- worth, Kans.; 1938 Ft. Riley, Kans.
Maj. Gen. Eugene Salet Augusta, Ga. Born Standish, Calif.	1929 Ft. Douglas, Utah
Lt. Col. Louis ("Gene") Schueler, USAF Prairie du Chien, Wis. Born Superior, Wis.	1935 Ft. McCoy, Wis.
Maj. Arnold Silver, USAF Charlotte, N.C. Born Carlisle, S.C.	1933–1934 Ft. Oglethorpe, Ga.
Col. Eugene Small Fairfax, Va. Born New York, N.Y.	1937 Ft. Dix, N.J.
William Snell, M.D. Pebble Beach, Calif. Born Arlington, Ore.	1937–1940 Vancouver Brks., Wash. Commissioned through CMTC
Maj. F. Thomas Steele Port Charlotte, Fla. Born Philadelphia, Pa.	1936 Ft. Meade, Md. 1937–1939 Ft. Hoyle, Md.
Capt. Archie Stewart San Antonio, Tex. Born Dallas, Tex.	1936 Ft. Sill, Okla.
Col. Robert Sumner Tampa, Fla. Born Portland, Ore.	1938–1940 Vancouver Brks., Wash.
Dave Taylor Richland, Wash. Born Great Falls, Mont.	1935–1937, 1939 Ft. George Wright, Wash.
Marco Thorne San Diego, Calif. Born Los Angeles, Calif.	1931 Del Monte, Monterey, Calif. 1932–1935 Presidio of Monterey, Calif.
Col. Harry Traffert, USMCR Long Beach, Calif. Born St. Louis, Mo.	1921 Camp Pike, Ark. 1922 Jefferson Brks., Mo. 1923–1924 Ft. Des Moines, Iowa 1925 Ft. Snelling, Minn.

Lt. Col. Dirk van der Voet
Charlottesville, Va.
Born Hudson, N.H.

1938 Ft. McKinley, Maine
1939–1940 Ft. Ethan Allen, Vt.
Commissioned through CMTC

Maj. Joseph Watts
Alexandria, Va.
Born Pittsburgh, Pa.

1939–1940 Ft. Ord, Calif.

Col. Earl ("Buck") Weaver
Hampton, Va.
Born Sheboygan, Wis.

1936–1938, Camp McCoy, Wis.

CWO P. L. Wells, USN
Grand Cane, La.
Born Shreveport, La.

1929 Ft. Leavenworth, Kans.
1930 Jefferson Brks., Mo.
1931–1932 Camp Beauregard, La.

Robert Wentworth
Braintree, Mass.
Born Boston, Mass.

1929 Ft. Devens, Mass.
1930–1932 Ft. McKinley, Maine
Commissioned through CMTC

Lt. Col. Edgar ("Ned") Wiencke,
USAF
Annapolis, Md.
Born Baltimore, Md.

1935 Ft. Monroe, Va.

Capt. Robert Williamson, USNR
Dallas, Tex.
Born Minneapolis, Minn.

1928 Ft. Hoyle, Md.

Henry Grady Young
Mt. Pleasant, Tex.
Born Waco, Tex.

1934–1936 Ft. Sill, Okla.

M. Sgt. John Yount, USAF
Pittsburgh, Pa.
Born Verona, Pa.

1940 Fort Meade, Md.

Bibliographic Essay and Acknowledgments

For my basic research I principally relied on the San Francisco Public Library since I live 3,000 miles from the founding grounds of the Plattsburg Movement, the Military Training Camps Association (MTCA), and Citizens' Military Training Camps itself. What the San Francisco Library could furnish was considerable. Its collection of the Secretary of War's annual reports from 1915 through 1941 provided CMTC annual attendance and budget figures. Also the library's New York Times index and microfilm collection of daily editions for the same period revealed more detail on CMTC than could possibly be used.

A matchless single source was John Garry Clifford's *The Citizen Soldiers: The Plattsburg Training Camp Movement, 1913–1920,* as this book's endnotes indicate. I am also indebted to Mr. Clifford for his review of my manuscript and helpful suggestions.

The U.S. Army Military History Institute at Carlisle Barracks, Pennsylvania, was a prolific source of articles on CMTC from military journals of the period. Through the generous cooperation of John Slonaker and Louis Arnold-Friend of the Historical Reference Branch, I was able to acquire all the material by correspondence. Their help was equivalent to my having personally visited Carlisle Barracks.

Bernard C. Nalty, a retired historian with the U.S. Air Force history program, was my first source for research materials on CMTC (Colored). He helped me locate a research assistant in Washington, D.C., and later reviewed the entire manuscript, making cogent suggestions. I was fortunate to be able to locate a friend and former boss from my service in Vietnam, Col. Felix Goodwin, who told me of Lt. Col. Charles M. Bussey and his book *Firefight at Yechon.* Col. Goodwin put me in touch with Lt. Col. Bussey, who adds validity to the chapter on segregated CMTC.

A visit to the National Archives capped off my research. Mitchell Yockelson, archivist in the Military Reference Branch, went out of his way to provide support during my three-day visit. He also cheerfully came to my assistance on several occasions after I had returned to California. Aimee Turner, research assistant, spent a whole day at the Archives' Suitland Annex digging up valuable material on CMTC (Colored) that became the heart of Chapter 22. Although the National Archives' CMTC files were copious and far more comprehensive than I could use, there was one disappointing gap in them. The collection of annual reports from the nine U.S. Army corps areas was incomplete and spotty. A complete set of corps area annual reports for CMTC's 20-year period would have provided details on specific camp attendance and the location of camps for each year. That information is apparently lost to history.

The authoritative sources for contemporary news events, motion pictures, popular songs, and radio programs came almost entirely from four publications: *Chronicle of the 20th Century; This Fabulous Century: 1920–1930* and *1930–1940; Variety Music Cavalcade, 1620–1961, A Chronology of Vocal and Instrumental Music Popular in the United States,* by Julius Mattfeld; and *Radio's Golden Age: The Programs and the Personalities*, by Frank Buxton and Bill Owen.

The materials supplied me by the CMTC alumni who responded to my search were priceless. Many of the former CMTC candidates donated yearbooks, camp newspapers, corps area and individual camp documents, and local CMTC recruiting and promotion items—materials that I never would have uncovered otherwise.

Almost 200 individuals contributed directly to the writing of this book. But if in 1974 my good friend Fred Nichols hadn't sent me the Camp Knox 1925 *Mess Kit*, the subject of CMTC never would have come to my mind. Almost half of this story of CMTC is told by 93 alumni of the camps, each of whom is named in the book and listed alphabetically in the section titled "Names of CMTC Alumni Quoted." Obviously I am indebted to each of them for lending their memories to the account; but several of these former "CMTCers" deserve additional mention for the exceptional interest they showed and contributions they made to the development of this history of CMTC. Without Maj. Gen. David Gray's having urged me to begin the book immediately rather than waiting until retirement, I would have been still in the research phase at the time I completed the project. Marco Thorne, a retired chief librarian, gave me early help on valuable bibliographic sources.

Richard Matteson, D.V.M., made my job easier with his ongoing interest, encouragement, and supply of background materials. Bill Bentson contributed not only many interesting anecdotes, but also supplied more than 20 names of CMTC alumni. Fred Featherstone also provided additional names, several of whom sent in valuable CMTC memories. Although not quoted in the book, CMTC alumnus Frank Sternard provided great assistance by examining the archives of the MTCA at the Chicago Historical Society. A CMTC alumnus, Lt. Col. William Clifford White, of Valley Station, Kentucky, must not go unmentioned; he was one of my early contacts in 1975 and was the alumni chairman for the 50th anniversary reunion at Fort Knox.

I am indebted to my good friends, Anita and Ernest Scott, for their professional guidance and work in the production of this book. Hal and Robin Lockwood, owners and operators of Penmarin Books, were also of great assistance in several stages of production. Rosaleen Bertolino, copy editor for the book, went "above and beyond" her professional responsibilities in making the book as readable as possible. I thank my wife, Jo Ann Mills Kington, for her patience and interest, as well as her sharp eye in making corrections in and suggestions on the manuscript. Daughter, Kimmel Kington, also made several valuable suggestions for improvements in early drafts. Our other daugher, Ann Kington Friedland, used her professional eye to catch many needed corrections in the final proofs.

Nearly 90 other CMTC alumni returned completed questionnaires and, although they are not quoted in the book, they added to my understanding and appreciation of the entire 20 years of CMTC. They are:* George Alexander, Newberg, Ore.; William Allen, San Francisco, Calif.; Lt. Col. Eugene Baird, Clearwater, Fla.; Lt. Cmdr. James Barto, USNR, Pittsburgh, Pa.; Lt. Col. Charles Baugn, USAF, Flemington, N.J.; Lt. Col. Donald Bockbrader, Dallas, Tex.; M. Sgt. Ben Breen, USAFR, San Jose, Calif.; Brig. Gen. Ralph Briggs, Waterford, Conn.; CWO Robert Briggs, Trumbull, Conn.; Paul Burrows, Seattle, Wash.; Col. Henry Calder, Dallas, Tex.; Frank Catanzarite, Rancho Palos Verdes, Calif.; Don Chalmers, Troutdale, Ore.; Col. Lynn Chamberlain, Carlsbad, Calif.; Lt. Col. Merritt Chesnut, USMCR, Palo Alto, Calif.; Col. Tom Cole, Cota de Casa, Calif.; Judge Andrew Conlyn (Col., National Guard), Kilmarnock, Va.; Col. Miles Connor, USAF, San

---

*Those who are listed with a military rank are retired and were in the U.S. Army unless another branch of service is listed.

Antonio, Tex.; Sandy Cortesio, Centerville, Iowa; 1st Lt. D. J. Costigan, Lansdowne, Pa.; Walter Craig, North Little Rock, Ark.; G. William Curtis, San Diego, Calif.; Lt. Col. Lawrence Desmond, Vallejo, Calif.; Lou Diov, Lodi, N.J.; Maj. Daniel Donahue, USAF, Suisun, Calif.; Lt. Col. Edward Donlon, Virginia Beach, Va.; Maj. Sol Fenichel, Ft. Lauderdale, Fla.; Raymond Fletcher, Ph.D., Garland, Tex.; Albert Frechette, Milan, N.H.; Lt. Col. Lowell Fricke, Poteau, Okla.; Mrs. James Gemmel (completed the questionnaire in the name of her late husband), Salem, Ore.; CWO Tom Giordano, Bloomfield, N.Y.; Sfc. Perry Greenberg, El Paso, Tex.; Lt. Col. Carl Griffin, El Paso, Tex.; Earl Griffith, Lakewood, Colo.; Maj. Richard Harris, USAF, Albuquerque, N.M.; Col. Aram ("Harry") Hatch, Lillian, Ala.; Loren Hicks, Salem, Ore.; John Huntoon, Honolulu, Hawaii; Lt. Col. George Isenberg, Oakdale, Calif.; Homer Jamison, D.D., Birmingham, Ala.; M. Chief PO Russell Jamison, USN, Sanford, Fla.; Lt. Col. Lyle Jones, USAF, Stuart, Fla.; Command Sgt. Maj. V. J. Jurgaitis, Philadelphia, Pa.; Col. Karl Landstrom, Arlington, Va.; Lt. Col. Elwood Luellen, Bradenton, Fla.; Capt. Byrd Lyon, USAF, Augusta, Ga.; Col. J. J. McAleer, Brookfield, Conn.; Lt. Col. John McCormick, Bedford, Va.; Maj. Walter McEnaney, Windsor, Vt.; Dr. Laurence McGonagle, (Lt. Col., Army Med. Corps), San Antonio, Tex.; Earl Mahan, Brisbane, Queensland, Australia; Col. Armen Mardiros, Orinda, Calif.; Henry Mourning, Lynchburg, Va.; William Mudd, Menlo Park, Calif.; Lt. Col. Jerald Mulkey, Salem, Ore.; Lt. Col. John Osborne, Napa, Calif.; Lt. Col. Earl Otis, Auburn, Calif.; Dr. Erwin Palmer, Oswego, N.Y.; Sgt. Maj. Sidney Platt, USMC, St. Stephen, S.C.; Philip Povey, Foster City, Calif.; Arthur Reibe, Metairie, La.; Norman Reitz, Moorhead, Minn.; Col. Harry Roller, Anacoco, La.; David Rolston, Northbrook, Ill.; Walter Rose, Alexandria, Va.; M. Sgt. Harry Rucker, Springville, N.Y.; Donald Saville, Berlin, Md.; Lt. Robert Schneider, San Diego, Calif.; Capt. Raymond Seddon, Harwinton, Conn.; Sgt. Maj. William Shrenk, Paso Robles, Calif.; Lt. Col. James Sikes, Grandin, Fla.; Lt. Col. Cecil Smith, Prairie du Chien, Wis.; Lt. Col. John Solomon, Carefree, Ariz.; Maj. Howard Spinning, Auburn, Calif.; Sfc. Robley Stearnes, Salem, Va.; WO Everett Tatro, USAF, Santa Cruz, Calif.; Col. Edgar Tidwell, San Diego, Calif.; Alan Toole, Spokane, Wash.; Lt. Col. Donald Turnbull, Portland, Ore.; Don Turner, Salem, Ore.; James Walsh, Cincinnati, Ohio; M. Sgt. Vernon Welch, USAF, Parker, Fla.; Lt. Col. Henry Williams, USAFR, Camden, S.C.; Lt. Col. Clark Wilson, USAF, Colorado Springs, Colo.; Richard Wing, Folsom, Calif.; Stanley Wolczyk, Wadsworth, Ohio; and Lt. Gen. John Wright, Jr., Irving, Texas.

Bibliography

BOOKS

Allen, Frederick Lewis. *Only Yesterday: An Informal History of the Nineteen-Twenties.* Harper Brothers, New York. 1931.

Allen, Frederick Lewis. *Since Yesterday: The 1930s in America, Sept. 3, 1929–Sept. 3, 1939.* Harper & Row, New York. 1939.

Bussey, Charles M. *Firefight at Yechon: Courage and Racism in the Korean War.* Brassey's, New York. 1991.

Buxton, Frank, and Bill Owen. *Radio's Golden Age: The Programs and the Personalities.* Easton Valley Press, New York. 1966.

Cannon, Lou. *Reagan.* C. D. Putnam Sons, New York. 1982.

Carlton, John T., and John F. Slinkman. *The ROA Story.* Reserve Officers' Assoc. of the U.S., Washington, D.C. 1982.

Chronicle of the 20th Century. Chronicle Publications, Mount Kisco, N.Y. 1987.

Clifford, John Garry. *The Citizen Soldiers: The Plattsburg Training Camp Movement, 1913–1920.* University Press of Kentucky, Lexington, Ky. 1972.

Clifford, John Garry, and Samuel R. Spencer, Jr. *The First Peacetime Draft.* University Press of Kansas, Lawrence, Kans. 1986.

Creamer, Robert W. *Baseball in '41.* Viking Press, New York. 1991.

Crossland, Richard A., and James T. Currie. *Twice the Citizen: A History of the United States Army Reserve, 1908–1983.* Office of the Chief, Army Reserve, Washington, D.C. 1984.

Edwards, Anne. *Early Reagan.* William Morrow, New York. 1987.

Frye, William. *Marshall, Citizen Soldier.* Bobbs-Merrill, Indianapolis, Ind. 1947.

Gann, Ernest K. *A Hostage to Fortune.* Alfred A. Knopf, New York. 1978.

Grimshaw, James A., Jr. *Robert Penn Warren: A Descriptive Bibliography, 1922–79.* University Press of Virginia, Charlottesville, Va. 1981.

Hill, Jim Dan. *The Minute Men in Peace and War: A History of the National Guard.* Telegraph Press, Harrisburg, Pa. 1964.

Lane, Jack C. *Armed Progressive, General Leonard Wood.* Presidio Press, San Rafael, Calif. 1978.

Manchester, William Raymond. *American Caesar, Douglas MacArthur, 1880–1964.* Little, Brown, Boston. 1978.

Mattfeld, Julius. *Variety Music Cavalcade, 1620–1961: A Chronology of Vocal and Instrumental Music Popular in the United States.* Prentice-Hall, Englewood Cliffs, N.J. 1962.

Mattloff, Maurice. *American Military History.* Office of the Chief of Military History, U.S. Army, Washington, D.C. 1969.

Millis, Walter. *Road to War.* Houghton Mifflin, Boston. 1935.

Mosley, Leonard. *Marshall, Hero for Our Times.* Hearst Books, New York. 1982.

Nason, Leonard H. *The Top Kick.* Doubleday, Doran and Co., Garden City, N.Y., 1928.

Reagan, Ronald. *An American Life: Ronald Reagan's Autobiography.* Simon & Schuster, New York. 1990.

Roberts, Cecil E. *A Soldier from Texas.* Branch-Smith, Fort Worth, Tex. 1978.

Rumer, Thomas A., *The American Legion: An Official History, 1919–1989.* M. Evans & Co., New York. 1990.

Seldes, George, comp. *The Great Quotations.* Pocket Books, New York. 1970.

Smythe, Donald. *Pershing, General of the Armies.* Indiana University Press, Bloomington, Ind. 1986.

Talese, Gay. *The Kingdom and the Power.* World Publishing, Cleveland, Ohio. 1966.

This Fabulous Century: 1920–1930 and *1930–1940.* Time-Life Books, New York. 1969.

Villard, Oswald G. *Our Military Chaos: The Truth about Defense.* Knopf, New York. 1939.

Vogel, Victor. *Soldiers of the Old Army.* Texas A & M University Press, College Station, Tex. 1990.

Weigley, Russell F. *History of the United States Army.* Macmillan, New York. 1967.

PERIODICALS

Barnes, Capt. Harry C., Jr., USA. "Vacations on Uncle Sam." *Sunset Magazine* (July 1928): pp. 34–37.

Bentson, Maj. William A., AUS. "Pre-WWII Patriots 'Forgotten Corps.'" *The Officer* (The Reserve Officer Association) (July 1986): pp. 30–32.

Brown, Maj. Gen. Preston, USA. "The Genesis of the Military Training Camps." *Infantry Journal.* (December 1930): pp. 609–13.

Caygill, Capt. H. W., USA. "CMTC Recruiting." *Infantry Journal* (November 1922): pp. 535–40.

Davis, R. C. "Good Citizenship Training Aim of Citizens' Military Training Camps." *School Life* (Dept. of the Interior, Bureau of Education) (April 1925): pp. 141–43.

Dill, Capt. L. C., USA. "Administration of a C.M.T. Camp." *Infantry Journal* (April 1926): pp. 388–96.

Esquire: Fiftieth Anniversary Collector's Issue: How We Lived, 1933–1983 (June 1983).

Fleet, Lt. Col. H. W., USA. "Citizens' Military Training Camps." *Infantry Journal* (May 1928): pp. 492–99.

Hamilton, Lt. Cdr. Maxwell, USN. "They Called Us Cannon Fodder." *TROA Magazine* (The Retired Officers' Association) (July 1985): pp. 24–28.

Hammond, J. J. "Crusaders Spread Gospel of Health, Ethics and Patriotism." *School Life* (Dept. of the Interior, Bureau of Education) (May 1927): pp. 167–69.

Luberoff, Maj. George, QMC. "Preparation of Summer Camps." *The Quartermaster Review* (March–April 1931): pp. 27–29.

McCaffrey, Lt. Gen. William J., USA. "Gen. Van Fleet: One of the Last the Stars Fell On." *Army* (December 1992): pp. 8; 10–11.

"A Message to Parents of High School Boys: What the CMTC Offers YOUR Son," *U.S. Army Recruiting News* (April 15, 1935): p. 6.

Ney, Lt. Virgil, Inf. Reserve. "The C.M.T.C. Instructor." *Infantry Journal* (May–June 1932): pp. 201–3.

Paisley, Lt. Col. Oldham, Inf. Reserve. "Citizenship Training in Citizen [*sic*] Military Training Camps." *Infantry Journal* (November–December 1933): p. 443.

Pershing, John J. "Peace-Time Patriotism," *Woman's Home Companion* (July 1924): pp. 4; 60.

Phillipson, I. J. "Citizens' Military Training Camps Receive Commendation." *School Life* (Dept. of the Interior, Bureau of Education) (May 1926): pp. 164–66.

Schick, Lt. Robert, AG, Reserve. "Advantages of the CMTC: Training in Citizenship Combined with Program of Wholesome Physical Development." *U.S. Army Recruiting News* (July 1940): pp. 6; 14.

Steward, Col. M. B., USA. "The Training Camps and Their Purposes." *Infantry Journal* (October 1921): pp. 368–76.

Waldron, Col. W. H. "CMTC Enrollment." *Infantry Journal* (October 1927): pp. 418–20.

Wentworth, Maj. Robert B., USAF (Ret.). "Its Regiments Never Fought." *VFW Magazine* (February 1984): pp. 46–47; 66.

CMTC CAMP YEARBOOKS

Barracks Bag. Ft. Snelling, Minn., 1924.

Citizens [sic] *Military Training Camp, Red Course.* Ft. Snelling, Minn., 1921.

Citizens' Military Training Camps 1930, Michigan, published by MTCA.

History of Michigan Camps 1929, published by MTCA.

The Mess Kit. Camp Knox, Ky. 1922, published by MTCA.

The Mess Kit. Camp Knox, Ky. 1923, published by MTCA.

The Mess Kit. Camp Knox, Ky. 1925, published by MTCA.

The Patriot. Ft. Ethan Allen, Vt., 1940.

Reveille to Taps. Plattsburg, N.Y., 1922.

CMTC CAMP NEWSPAPERS

The Howitzer. Madison Brks., N.Y.

The Little Bearcat. Presidio of Monterey, Calif.

Rangefinder. Madison Brks., N.Y.

The Salvo. Ft. Monroe, Va.

Tumbleweed Pick-ups. Ft. Sill, Okla.

GOVERNMENT AND ASSOCIATION DOCUMENTS

ARMY REGULATIONS No. 350-2900, Dec. 15, 1938. War Department, Washington, D.C.

Camp Regulations for C.M.T.C. Candidates, 1939. Fort Dix, N.J. (photocopy donated to author by CMTC alumnus.)

Citizens' Military Training Camps. First Corps Area, 1935. (pamphlet. original copy in author's files, donated by CMTC alumnus.)

Citizens' Military Training Camps. Ninth Corps Area, 1939. (pamphlet. photocopy donated to author by CMTC alumnus.)

Citizens' Military Training Camps. Third Corps Area, 1931. (pamphlet. photocopy donated to author by CMTC alumnus.)

Citizens' Military Training Camps: Extract from Proceedings of the Twenty-Ninth Annual Encampment of the Veterans of Foreign Wars of the United States at Indianapolis, Ind., August 16–31, 1928. (Library of Congress. photocopy donated to author by CMTC alumnus.)

Citizens' Military Training Camps: Red, White, and Blue Courses. U.S. Government Printing Office, Washington, D.C., 1921. (Library of Congress. photocopy donated to author by CMTC alumnus.)

C.M.T.C.–Training Camps for Young Men. Fifth Corps Area pamphlet, 1935. (photocopy donated to author by CMTC alumnus.)

Eleven Years of the CMTC: A Brief Account of the Citizens' Military Training Camps, 1921–1931. published by MTCA. (original in author's files, donated by CMTC alumnus.)

Fourth Corps Area 1938 C.M.T.C. Information Pamphlet. (original in author's files, donated by CMTC alumnus.)

"History of CMTC." (mimeographed, undated, unsigned brief paper in author's files.)

"History of the Secretary of the Army's Civilian Aide Program." (mimeographed, undated, unsigned paper in author's files.)

Infantry Drill Regulations. Field Manual 22-5, July 1, 1939, War Department, Washington, D.C. (U.S. Army Military History Institute, Carlisle Brks., Pa.)

Information Regarding Citizens' Military Training Camps. Third Corps Area, 1939. (photocopy donated to author by CMTC alumnus.)

Information and Regulations CMTC, Camp Devens, Mass., 1922. (photocopy donated to author by CMTC alumnus.)

Let's Pull Together for the C.M.T.C. Civilian Military Education Fund, Washington, D.C., 1938. (original copy in author's files, donated by CMTC alumnus.)

The Military Training Camps Association of the United States. pamphlet published by MTCA, 1935. (original in author's files, donated by CMTC alumnus.)

SPECIAL REGULATIONS No.44b, 1921. War Department, Washington, D.C. (U.S. Army Military History Institute, Carlisle Brks., Pa.)

The Story of the Camps. MTCA, Chicago. 1925. (U.S. Army Military History Institute, Carlisle Brks., Pa.)

Tentative Infantry Drill Regulations, 1932. War Department, Washington, D.C. (U.S. Army Military History Institute, Carlisle Brks., Pa.)

This Is Great! The Citizens' Military Training Camps. pamphlet, apparently published by U.S. Government in 1935. (photocopy donated to author by CMTC alumnus.)

Trainee's Manual C.M.T.C. Camp Custer, Mich., 1940. (photocopy donated to author by CMTC alumnus.)

War Department Annual Report, Fiscal Years 1917, 1918, and 1921 through 1924. War Department, Washington, D.C. (San Francisco Main Library.)

What Parents Think of the Citizens' Military Training Camps. Hqs. Ninth Corps Area, Presidio of San Francisco, 1924. (National Archives.)

UNPUBLISHED MATERIAL

Ryan, Col. William A. Article on his father's experience at Ft. Snelling, Minn., CMTC in 1921. (copy furnished to author of this book by Col. Ryan.)

McCann, Francis W. Letters written from Camp Devens, Mass., to his parents, 1921. (furnished to the author of this book by his son, John C. McCann.)

Salet, Maj. Gen. Eugene. Unpublished memoirs. undated. (portions provided to the author of this book by Gen. Salet.)

★ ★ ★

Notes

The following abreviations are used in the notes. See the bibliography for complete pubication information for the works cited here.

WD — *War Department*
NYT — *New York Times*
Mess Kit — *The Mess Kit* (CMTC yearbook)

CHAPTER 1

1. See Jack C. Lane. *Armed Progressive, General Leonard Wood.*
2. *WD Annual Reports, 1912.* p. 121.
3. Brown, Maj. Gen. Preston, USA. "The Genesis of the Military Training Camps." *Infantry Journal.* (December 1930): p. 609.
4. Clifford, John Garry. *The Citizen Soldiers.* p. 12.
5. Ibid. p. 16.
6. Ibid. pp. 25–26.
7. Ibid. pp. 72–73.
8. *Mess Kit.*1923. p. 13.
9. Clifford. *The Citizen Soldiers.* Chapter IV, p. 92.
10. *WD Annual Reports, 1918.* p. 121.
11. Ibid. p. 183.
12. Ibid. pp. 19; 189.
13. Nason, Leonard H. *The Top Kick.* p. 10.
14. Clifford. *The Citizen Soldiers.* Chapter VII, p. 193.

CHAPTER 2

1. McCann, Francis W. Letters to his parents. Furnished by his son, John C. McCann.

2. Ryan, William A. Unpublished article on his father's experience at Ft. Snelling, Minn., CMTC in 1921.

3. *WD Annual Reports, 1922.* p. 192.

4. Special Regulation 44b. 1921. par. 27, p. 12. (Section 47d of the 1920 ammendment reprented, in part in Special Regulation 44b.)

5. Ibid. par. 1, p. 5.

6. Ibid. Sect. III, pp. 12–15.

7. *WD Annual Reports, 1921.* p. 31

8. *NYT.* March 25, 1921. p. 19.

9. *WD Annual Reports, 1922.* p. 192.

10. *San Francisco Examiner.* July 10, 1921.

11. *NYT.* June 13, 1921. p. 15.

12. *NYT.* Aug. 16, 1921. p. 17.

13. *Mess Kit.* 1922. p. 7.

14. *WD Annual Reports, 1922.* p. 191.

15. Ibid. p. 192.

16. 1921 CMTC Yearbook. Ft. Snelling. p. 27.

CHAPTER 3

1. *NYT Index, 1921.*

2. Talese, Gay. *The Kingdom and the Power.* pp. 174–75; 214. *NYT.* April 27, 1932. p. 38.

3. Caygill, Capt. H. W., USA. "CMTC Recruiting." *Infantry Journal* (November 1922): p. 535.

4. Ibid. p. 536.

5. Ibid.

6. Ibid.

7. Ibid. p. 537.

8. *WD Annual Reports, 1922.* p. 192.

9. Ibid.

10. Caygill, "CMTC Recruiting." p. 539.

11. *Mess Kit,* 1925. p. 177.

12. *WD Annual Reports, 1923.*

13. Ibid. p. 153.

14. *San Francisco Examiner.* July 9, 1922. p. 4.

15. *NYT Index, 1922.*

16. *NYT.* Aug. 3, 1922. p. 14.

17. *NYT.* Aug. 6, 1922. p. 10.

18. *NYT.* Aug. 20, 1922. Sect. VII; p. 5.

19. *NYT.* Aug. 22, 1922. p. 10.
20. *Mess Kit.* 1922. p. 148. This is the yearbook where Robert Penn Warren's poem appeared (p. 41).
21. Ibid. pp. 80–81.
22. Ibid. p. 126.
23. Ibid. p. 146.

CHAPTER 4
1. Special Regulation 44b. 1921. par 8, pp. 6–7.
2. Ibid. par. 42. pp. 17–18.
3. *WD Annual Reports, 1922.* p. 192.
4. *San Francisco Call & Post.* July 6, 1922.
5. *Mess Kit, 1922.* pp. 70–84.

CHAPTER 5
1. *Mess Kit, 1922.* p. 149.

CHAPTER 6
1. Vogel, Victor. *Soldiers of the Old Army.* p. 32.

CHAPTER 7
1. *Mess Kit.* 1925. p. 128.
2. Ibid. p. 150.
3. *NYT.* Aug. 5, 1924. p. 40.

CHAPTER 8
1. Special Regulation 44b. par. 23. p. 11.
2. *San Francisco Chronicle.* July 7, 1922. p. 4.
3. *San Francisco Call & Post.* July 7, 1922. p. 5.
4. *Mess Kit.* 1925. p. 91.
5. Ibid. p. 183.
6. Salet, Eugene, Maj. Gen., USA (Ret.). Unpublished memoirs. undated. Provided to the author of this book by Maj. Gen. Salet.
7. *Mess Kit.* 1925. p. 103.
8. See Crossland, Richard A. and James T. Currie. *Twice the Citizen: A History of the United States Army Reserve, 1908–1983.*

CHAPTER 9
1. Army Regulation 350-2200. Dec. 15, 1938. par. 10, pp. 4–5.

2. Ibid.
3. Ibid.
4. *Mess Kit.* 1925. p. 179.
5. *Mess Kit.* 1922. p. 148
6. Roberts, Cecil E. *A Soldier from Texas.* Branch-Smith, Inc., Fort Worth, Tex., 1978. p. 8.
7. *NYT.* July 12, 1937. p. 12.

CHAPTER 10

1. WD *Annual Reports, 1924.* pp. 162–63.
2. *NYT.* July 1, 1923. p. 5.
3. *NYT.* Aug 17, 1923. p. 2.
4. *NYT.* July 15, 1923. Sect II, p. 2.
5. *NYT.* July 15, 1923. p. 1.
6. *NYT.* July 17, 1923. p. 18.
7. *NYT.* Aug. 26, 1923. p. 13.
8. *NYT.* Aug. 28, 1923. p. 6.
9. *NYT.* July 25, 1923. p. 26. Also see Clifford, *The Citizen Soldiers,* and Clifford and Spencer, *The First Peacetime Draft.*
10. *NYT.* Aug. 14, 1923. p. 16: *NYT* Aug. 17, 1923. p. 2.
11. *NYT.* Aug. 19, 1923. p. 17.
12. *NYT.* Aug. 15, 1923. p. 24.
13. *NYT.* July 28, 1923. p. 9.
14. *NYT.* July 27, 1923. p. 13.
15. *NYT.* Aug. 30, 1921. p. 17.
16. *NYT.* July 24, 1921. p. 17.
17. Letter from the Adjutant General, War Department, Feb. 14, 1924. Subject: Special Training Companies. Quoted in *NYT* Sep. 16, 1923. p. 1.
18. *NYT.* Aug. 13, 1923. p. 1.

CHAPTER 11

1. "C.M.T.C.Training Camps for Young Men," Fifth Corps Area pamphlet, 1935.
2. Salet. Unpublished memoirs.
3. Hamilton, Lt. Cdr. Maxwell, USN (Ret.). "They Called Us Cannon Fodder." *TROA Magazine* (July 1985): p. 26.
4. Special Order 100, Ft. Meade, Md. July 13.
5. Ibid.
6. Ibid.

7. *NYT.* July 19, 1940. p. 30.
8. *Barracks Bag.* Ft. Snelling, Minn. 1924 yearbook. (pages unnumbered)
9. *This Fabulous Century—1920–1930.* pp. 268–69.
10. *NYT.* Aug. 26, 1926. p. 8.
11. *NYT.* July 24, 1935. p. 19.
12. *Mess Kit.* 1925. p. 110.

CHAPTER 13

1. *WD Annual Reports, 1924.* p 12.
2. Ibid.
3. Davis, R. C. "Good Citizenship Training Aim of Citizens' Military Training Camps." *School Life* (April 1925): p. 141.
4. *NYT.* Aug. 8, 1924. p. 12.
5. *Barracks Bag.* Ft. Snelling, Minn., 1924 yearbook. Advertising section. (pages unnumbered)
6. Ibid.
7. *Mess Kit.* 1925. p. 183.
8. Allen, Frederick Lewis. *Only Yesterday: An Informal History of the Nineteen-Twenties.* p. 162.
9. Ibid. p. 102.
10. *Mess Kit.* 1925. p. 77.
11. *Barracks Bag.* Ft. Snelling. 1924. Co. C article.
12. *WD Annual Reports, 1925.* p. 45.
13. Ibid.
14. Ibid. p. 183.

CHAPTER 14

1. Vogel. *Soldiers of the Old Army.* p. 48.
2. *Mess Kit.* 1922. p. 125.
3. Ibid. p. 135.
4. *Barracks Bag.* Ft. Snelling. 1924. Co. H "Cavalry of 1924."
5. *Mess Kit.* 1925. p. 95.
6. *NYT.* Aug. 24, 1932. p. 17.
7. Gann, Ernest K. *A Hostage to Fortune.* p. 69.

CHAPTER 15

1. *NYT.* July 1, 1926. p. 14. Army Regulation 350-2200. par. 41. p. 18.
2. *WD Annual Reports, 1927.* p 56.
3. *NYT.* July 11, 1925. Sect. VIII, p. 18.

4. *NYT.* June 8, 1926. p. 42.
5. *NYT.* May 20, 1926. p. 14.
6. *NYT.* Aug. 2, 1926. p. 9
7. Smythe, Donald. *Pershing, General of the Armies.* p. 285.
8. *NYT.* July 22, 1926. p. 10.
9. *NYT.* Aug. 30, 1926. p. 32.
10. Ibid.
11. *WD Annual Reports, 1928.* p 232.
12. Ibid. p. 24.
13. Ibid. pp. 14–15.
14. Allen. *Only Yesterday.* p. 217.
15. Gann. *A Hostage to Fortune.* p. 67.
16. Allen. *Only Yesterday.* p. 216.
17. *NYT.* July 3, 1927. Sect. II, p. 1.
18. *NYT.* Aug. 9, 1927. p. 1.
19. *NYT.* Sept. 5, 1928. pp.3; 5.
20. *WD Annual Reports, 1929.* p. 107.
21. *NYT.* Aug. 10, 1928. p. 20.
22. *WD Annual Reports, 1930.* p 7.
23. *WD Annual Reports,* 1931. p. 241.

CHAPTER 16
1. Vogel. *Soldiers of the Old Army.* p. 16.
2. *The Salvo.* Ft. Monroe, Va., CMTC newspaper. July 6, 1939.
3. *Mess Kit,* 1925. p. 171.
4. Hamilton. "They Called Us Cannon Fodder." p. 27.
5. *The Howitzer.* Madison Barracks, N.Y. CMTC newspaper. Aug. 29, 1933.
6. *NYT.* July 12, 1929. p. 21.
7. *Tumbleweed Pick-ups.* Ft. Sill, Okla., CMTC newspaper. July 22, 1937.
8. *The Little Bearcat.* Presidio of Monterey, Calif., CMTC newspaper. Issues No. 2 and 3, July 1931.
9. *The Salvo.* Ft. Monroe, Va., CMTC newspaper. July 27, 1939.
10. *Mess Kit.* 1923. p. 146.
11. *Mess Kit.* 1925. p. 118.
12. *History of Michigan Camps 1929.* MTCA. p. 26. *Citizens' Military Training Camps 1930, Michigan.* MTCA. p. 42.

CHAPTER 17
1. Salet. Unpublished memoirs.
2. *Rangefinder.* Madison Barracks, N.Y., CMTC newspaper. July 13, 1940.

CHAPTER 18
1. *WD Annual Reports, 1932.* p. 24.
2. Mattfeld. *Variety Music Cavalcade.* p. 468. *Chronicle of the 20th Century.* p. 390.
3. *NYT.* Jan. 20, 1932. p. 1; Jan. 27, 1932. p. 4; and Jan. 30, 1932. p. 1.
4. *NYT.* Jan. 24, 1933. p. 11.
5. *NYT.* June 17, 1933. p. 13.
6. *WD Annual Reports, 1934.* p. 195.
7. *WD Annual Reports, 1935.* p. 125.
8. *WD Annual Reports, 1934.* p. 145. *WD Annual Reports, 1935.* p. 125.
9. *NYT.* July 27, 1933. p. 3.
10. Harry S Truman Library, Independence, Mo.
11. Reagan, Ronald. *An American Life: Ronald Reagan's Autobiography.* p. 72. Edwards, Anne. *Early Reagan.* pp. 144–45.
12. Cannon, Lou. *Reagan.* p. 48.
13. *The Little Bearcat.* Presidio of Monterey, Calif., CMTC newspaper. Issues of 1931 and 1932.
14. For the unfortunate though amusing story see Creamer, Robert W. *Baseball in '41.* pp. 272–75.
15. *WD Annual Reports, 1936.* p. 93.

CHAPTER 19
1. *WD Annual Reports, 1928.* p. 233.
2. *WD Annual Reports, 1924.* p. 163. *WD Annual Reports, 1925.* p. 152. *WD Annual Reports, 1926.* p. 183.
3. *WD Annual Reports, 1928.* p. 233.
4. *WD Annual Reports, 1930.* p. 358.
5. Ibid. Also *WD Annual Reports, 1931.* p. 217. *WD Annual Reports, 1932.* p. 241.
6. In *The Citizen Soldiers,* p. 297, Clifford reports 4,630 having been commissioned by 1934. A footnote credits his source as R. H. Hill, "Reserve Policies and National Defense," *Infantry Journal* (January 1935): pp. 59–61. Sources available during research for this book failed to document a number this high.

7. Seldes, George (comp.). *The Great Quotations.* p. 606.

8. *WD Annual Reports, 1941.* p. 43.

9. *NYT.* Sept. 5, 1927. pp. 3; 5.

10. "C.M.T.C.—Training Camps for Young Men," Fifth Corps Area pamphlet, 1935.

11. *The Salvo.* Camp Meade, Md., CMTC newspaper. 1939.

CHAPTER 20

1. *Mess Kit.* 1922. p. 143.

2. Report of Investigation, Hqs. Presidio of Monterey, 1939. (National Archives)

3. McCaffrey, William J. "Gen. Van Fleet: One of the Last the Stars Fell On." *Army Magazine.* (Dec. 1992): pp. 8; 10–11.

4. Special Regulation 44b, 1921. par. 23, p. 11.

5. *Information and Regulations CMTC, Camp Devens, Mass., 1922.* (pamphlet)

CHAPTER 21

1. The 1940 U.S. Census shows Shamokin township with a population of 1,717.

2. *NYT Index 1922.* July–Sept. p. 490, and *1923* July–Sept. p. 500.

3. Letter, Office of the General of the Armies, April 14, 1923, to Honorable John F. Carew, M.C., New York City.

4. *NYT.* July 27, 1923. p. 13.

5. Special Regulation No. 44b. par. 21.

6. *What Parents Think of the Citizens' Military Training Camps.* Hqs., Ninth Corps Area, Presidio of San Francisco, 1924.

7. Letter G-1/5573, to Major General Andrew W. Brewster, Commanding First Corps Area, Army Base, Boston 9, Mass., Oct. 20, 1923, signed by John J. Pershing.

8. *WD Annual Reports 1924* pp. 162–63. *WD Annual Reports, 1925.* p. 152.

9. *Mess Kit,* 1922 and 1923.

10. Letter from Hqs., Ft. Benjamin Harrison, Ind., Oct. 26, 1923, to: The Adjutant General of the Army. Subject: Address to Reserve Officers Association at Indianapolis.

11. Letter from Hqs., Seventh Corps Area, Omaha, Neb., Oct. 18, 1923, to: The Adjutant General of the Army, Washington, D.C., with seven

inclosures [*sic*], number seven missing. Subject: National Guard Opposition to C.M.T.Camps.
12. Memo from Operations & Training Division, G-3, War Department. to the Adjutant General of the Army, April 7, 1923. Subject: Enlistment at C.M.T. Camps of Members of White Course (draft of official directive).
13. *The Barracks Bag*, Ft. Snelling, Minn., 1924 CMTC yearbook. (pages unnumbered)
14. *NYT*. May 28, 1926. p. 35.
15. *WD Annual Reports 1928*, p. 16.
16. *NYT*. April 5, 1933. p. 20. (The Yale scholarships were also mentioned on July 15, 1937, p. 9 and March 19, 1939, Sect III, p. 5.)
17. *WD Annual Reports, 1929*. p. 191.
18. See Rumer, Thomas A., *The American Legion, An Official History, 1919–1989*.
19. Carlton, John T., and John F. Slinkman. *The ROA Story*. pp. 54–55; 101; 121; 124; 131; 137; 143. Also see *Citizens' Military Training Camps, Extract from Proceedings of the Twenty-Ninth Annual Encampment of the Veterans of Foreign Wars of the United States at Indianapolis, Ind., August 16–31, 1928.*
20. *NYT*. April 15, 1927. p. 14.
21. Report on Essay Contest, The Citizens' Military Training Camps, 1936, National Patriotic Council, and letter from same organization to Hon. Harry Woodring, Sec. of War, Aug. 26, 1937. (National Archives)
22. *CMTC, Extract from Proceedings of the Twenty-Ninth Annual Encampment of the VFW*. p. 10.
23. *NYT*. April 26, 1932. p. 24.
24. Memo dated May 31, 1939, with code "E-100" at bottom of page. (National Archives)
25. Carlton and Slinkman. *The ROA Story*. p. 124.
26. Manchester, William Raymond. *American Caesar, Douglas MacArthur, 1880–1964*. p. 135.
27. The first mention of the annual Pershing Medals was found in the MTCA's booklet "Memoirs of the CITIZENS [*sic*] TRAINING CAMPS 1934." The medal and trip were sponsored by the Civilian Military Education Fund, apparently an adjunct of the MTCA. Also see *NYT,* April 7, 1937, p. 35: Dec. 10, 1937, p 13: April 7, 1940, p. 39.
28. Pershing, John J. "Peace-Time Patriotism." *Women's Home Companion.* (July 1924): p 4.

29. Hamilton. "They Called Us Cannon Fodder." *TROA Magazine* (July 1985): p. 25.

30. *NYT.* May 16, 1927, p. 1: May 25, 1929: June 28, 1934.

31. Hamilton. "They Called Us Cannon Fodder." p. 26.

32. *NYT.* Aug. 7, 1926, p. 11. In an editorial (Aug. 9, 1926, p. 14) the *Times* writer ridiculed the pamphlet and the three youths who "are themselves in need of a lot more training."

33. Allen. *Only Yesterday.* Chapter III, p. 15.

34. *CMTC, Extract from Proceedings of the Twenty-Ninth Annual Encampment of the VFW.* p. 10.

35. Ibid. The report stated: "In one corps area alone there were trained 4,187 men this year as compared with 4,872 men the previous year." The unnamed corps area would most likely have been the Second, First, or Third, in that order; however, the VFW's figures don't match any of the numbers reported by either *War Department Annual Reports, fiscal year 1928* or 1929.

36. *NYT.* April 14, 1928. p. 11.

37. *NYT.* Aug. 22, 1929. p. 19.

38. *NYT.* July 29, 1930. p. 12.

39. *NYT.* Aug. 27, 1933. p. 29.

CHAPTER 22

1. CMTC Index #29, 15640-25, 7/15/40, "*Discrimin agnst negroes in CMTC.* Need for broader opportunity. of service in national defense. Ltr fr *Stafford King,* Civln Aid to S/W for CMTC in Minn. 7/8/40. [*sic*]"

2. *The Crisis* (NAACP periodical), Vol 27. No. 4, Feb. 1924. p. 151.

3. CMTC annual report, 1923, Seventh Corps Area, Ft. Omaha, Neb.

4. *NYT.* April 6, 1927. p. 15.

5. Ibid.

6. *NYT.* April 7, 1927. p. 32.

7. Ibid. p. 18.

8. Heller, Joseph, *Catch 22.*

9. Seventh Corps Area report April 11, 1938. Ninth Corps Area report April 1938. Hqs. Third Corps Area, Baltimore, Md. letter Subject: Estimated number of candidates, by arms and courses, CMTC 1938. April 18, 1938. Third Corps Area report Feb. 24, 1939.

10. Ibid.

11. CMTC correspondence Index #27 (National Archives, Suitland Annex) 3/27/36, "Concurrent Training Camp. Ft. Howard, Md. Allotmt. of funds

for rhabilitatn. of CMTC for colored trainees [*sic*]." It would appear the letter arranged for establishing facilities for a *new* CMTC (Colored) at Ft. Howard.

12. Bussey, Charles M. *Firefight at Yechon.* p. 5
13. Ibid. p. 6.
14. Ibid. p. 7.
15. Ibid. p. 8.
16. Ibid. p. 12.

CHAPTER 23

1. Allen, Frederick Lewis. *Since Yesterday: The 1930s in America, Sept. 3, 1929–Sept. 3, 1939.* p. 247.
2. *NYT.* April 5, 1936. Sect. II, p. 1.
3. Allen. *Since Yesterday.* pp. 245–46.
4. Ibid. p. 247.
5. Mattfeld. *Variety Music Cavalcade.* p. 465.
6. *WD Annual Reports, 1938.* p. 4.
7. Ibid.
8. Ibid. pp 85–86.
9. Allen. *Since Yesterday*, p. 307. See pp. 305–11 for his complete description of the 1937–1938 recession.
10. Allen. *Since Yesterday.* p. 307.
11. *WD Annual Reports, 1939.* p. 88.
12. *Chronicle of the 20th Century.* p. 478.
13. Allen. *Since Yesterday.* pp. 327–29. *This Fabulous Century.* pp. 35–37.
14. Mosley, Leonard. *Marshall, Hero for Our Times.* pp. 45–46.
15. Frye, William. *Marshall, Citizen Soldier.* p. 185.
16. Letter from Hqs. Vancouver Barracks, Wash., Aug. 12, 1937, to: CG, Ninth Corps Area, Presidio of San Francisco, Calif. Subject: CMT Camp, Vancouver Barracks, 1937.
17. *NYT.* Jan. 6, 1939. p. 13.
18. *WD Annual Reports, 1940.* p. 63.
19. Allen. *Since Yesterday.* pp. 332–33.
20. *NYT.* Aug. 3, 1939. p. 12.
21. *NYT.* Aug. 1, 1940. p. 24.
22. *NYT.* May 23, 1939. p. 3.
23. *WD Annual Reports, 1941.* p. 137.
24. Ibid. p. 138. *NYT.* June 15, 1940. p. 10.
25. See Lane. *Armed Progressive, General Leonard Wood.*

26. WD *Annual Reports, 1941.* p. 137. *NYT.* June 15, 1940. p. 10.
27. *NYT.* July 6, 1940. p. 8.
28. *NYT.* July 20, 1940. p. 30.
29. See Clifford and Spencer. *The First Peacetime Draft.*
30. *NYT.* Sep. 28, 1940. p. 17.
31. WD *Annual Reports, 1941.* p. 75.

CHAPTER 24

1. Special Regulations No. 44b. 1921. par. 1. Par. 14 of the regulation stated that the purpose of the Blue Course (final year) was "to provide more advanced training...with a view to their appointment as officers in the Officers' Reserve Corps if found qualified."
2. *The Story of the Camps.* MTCA, Chicago, 1925. p. 7. This same document was used as the preface to the 1925 Camp Knox yearbook, *The Mess Kit,* and probably other 1925 CMTC yearbooks.
3. WD *Annual Reports 1924.* p. 122.
4. WD *Annual Reports 1930.* p. 153.
5. WD *Annual Reports 1934.* p. 53.
6. WD *Annual Reports 1935.* pp. 50, 51.
7. Carlton and Slinkman. *The ROA Story.* p. 124.
8. *NYT.* March 29, 1931. p. 6.
9. Carlton and Slinkman. *The ROA Story.* p. 109.
10. *NYT.* Jan. 25, 1933. p. 16.
11. *NYT.* Jan. 11, 1931. p. 26.
12. *NYT.* Jan. 24, 1933. p. 11.
13. *NYT.* Jan. 25, 1933. p. 16.
14. *NYT.* Jan. 24, 1933. p. 11.
15. *NYT.* June 1, 1926. pp. 1; 11: *NYT.* May 22, 1928. p. 28.
16. *NYT.* May 22, 1928. p. 15.
17. *NYT.* Nov. 7, 1930. p. 18.
18. Villard, Oswald G. *Our Military Chaos: The Truth about Defense.* pp. 139–40.
19. Millis, Walter. *Road to War.* pp. 94–95.
20. Clifford. *The Citizen Soldiers.* p. 298.
21. Letter from Hqs. Sixth Corps Area, Sept. 14, 1923, to: The Adjutant General of the Army. Subject: Utilization of Civilian Aides for C.M.T.C. Recruiting.
22. Crossland, Richard A., and James T. Currie. *Twice the Citizen.* p. 42.
23. Ibid. pp. 42–43.

24. Ibid.
25. Undated, unsigned brief paper on the history of CMTC. p. 4.
26. Wentworth, Maj. Robert B., USAF (Ret.). "Its Regiments Never Fought." *VFW Magazine*. (February 1984). p. 66. A positive reaction to CMTC similar to that expressed by the contributors to this history is found in Wentworth's article. Wentworth, himself a CMTC veteran, surveyed more than 300 CMTC alumni while preparing his article.
27. *Army Times*. June 8, 1981. p. 4.

Index

COLONEL DONALD M. KINGTON, AUS, Retired, a native of Madisonville, Kentucky, has been a retail merchant, a civil servant, a professional soldier, and a communicator for a large bank, but never the professional singer he trained to be at Northwestern University's School of Music. Now retired from all his former vocations, he researches and writes pieces on early twentieth-century military history, and sings as a hobby. He and his wife, Jo Ann Mills Kington, from Madisonville as well, now live in San Francisco. Their four grown children also have adopted California as their home.